W9-BBJ-367

Essay on Exoticism

POST-CONTEMPORARY
INTERVENTIONS
*Series Editors: Stanley Fish and
Fredric Jameson*

Essay on Exoticism

An Aesthetics of Diversity

by VICTOR SEGALEN

Translated and Edited by Yaël Rachel Schlick

Foreword by Harry Harootunian

DUKE UNIVERSITY PRESS

Durham & London 2002

Assistance for the translation was provided by the
French Ministry of Culture/Centre National du Livre.
© 2002 Duke University Press
All rights reserved
Printed in the United States of America on acid-free paper ∞
Typeset in Monotype Garamond by Tseng Information Systems, Inc.
Library of Congress Cataloging-in-Publication Data appear on
the last printed page of this book.

Contents

Foreword:
The Exotics of Nowhere

Charles Baudelaire defended dandyism as the "best element in human pride," commending the flaneur's attempt to "combat and destroy triviality" in the struggle with a social conformism that threatened to install homogeneity everywhere that industrial capitalism had established its regime in the nineteenth century. A half century later, Victor Segalen nominated exoticism as the candidate best suited to protect contemporary life from the relentless banality wrought by the transformation of capitalism into mass-society imperialism and colonialism. This transformation, in his eyes, reached a climax with the Great War and its aftermath. Like Baudelaire, Segalen privileged the poetic. But where Baudelaire, according to Walter Benjamin, employed the "technique of the putsch," eschewing the armature of allegory, often appearing as a poet willing to support any of the causes pursued by this class, Segalen, recalling the example of Mallarmé and the theory of *poésie pure,* built a "production on . . . (a) basic renunciation of all manifest experiences of . . . class. . . . These difficulties turn . . . poetry into an esoteric poetry."[1] By contrast, Baudelaire, for the most part, avoided the esoteric, and, even though the experiences refracted through his optic "nowhere derived from the production process, least of all in its advanced form—the industrial process," his work still bore the imprint of the historical moment in the figures of the "neurasthenic, of the big-city dweller, and of the customer."[2] For Segalen, writing in a time when financial capital already occupied the political economic horizon and imperialist powers competed madly to seize and colonize much of the globe outside of Euro-America, the appeal to exoticism promised to trade the vast unevenness of this moment for the poetic dream of aesthetic diversity and the fantasy of irreparable loss of what never was. Yet this very refusal of reference marked precisely how the poet, now driven by the noble ideal of art for art's sake, confronts language the way "the buyer faces the commodity on the market."[3]

In his poetic "Essay on Exoticism," an unfinished fragment attesting to the primacy of art in a world now mired in the mediocrity of the masses and an everyday life landlocked in repetitive routine, Segalen looked outwardly to "things," "to the 'external world,' to the Object in its entirety" that speaks and interpellates him, much like Benjamin's (and Marx's) empathic "soul of the commodity," whispering its seductions to a "poor wretch who passes a shop window containing beautiful and expressive things" and seeing in "everyone the buyer in whose hand and house it wants to nestle."[4] For Segalen, the exoticism he ascribes to things, to the "Object in its entirety," "by an instantaneous, continuous *translation* that would echo one's presence rather than blurt it out bluntly," "will perhaps . . . create a terrain where I feel completely at home." Convinced that such a transformation depended upon the form one employs—what he called "art's reason for being," the act of translating the object and making visible what had remained hidden in a subjectivistic recess mobilized the unredeemed promise of a metaphysics of presence and its authentication of the individual's immediate experience. In this way, Segalen's rewriting of the text of exoticism abandoned the act of realistic description that had impelled so many travelers and tourists in the past to report on the strangeness they had encountered and replaced it with one founded on the eliciting of sensation and "suggestion." It also disdained the performative exoticism of a Pierre Loti or Lafcadio Hearn.

Even before Segalen began to write down the thoughts that would constitute the posthumous *Essay on Exoticism,* an older exoticism was already in practice, stemming from ceaseless overseas exploration and economic expansion and its accompanying search for new sources of raw material, markets, and cheap labor. This exoticism followed the itinerary of capitalism as it migrated around the globe and often masked the violent seizure and colonial expropriation that was at the heart of its law of movement. Segalen had observed that this exoticist practice was based on the prospect of an elsewhere, driven by the novelty of geographic unfamiliarity but exemplified by intrepid travelers/tourists like Pierre Loti, the explorer Richard Burton, and the cultural misfit Lafcadio Hearn. It signified the primacy of the spatial dimension of capitalist expansion at the expense of its temporal workings and thus managed to displace and often efface the baneful effects of the actual deterritorialization and reterritorialization of land, labor, and capital that transformed and destroyed received cultures of reference to make them little more than outposts of Western civilization. This mode of exoticism was entirely committed to spatializing territories into fixed, static, and unchanging landscapes that existed in temporalities outside of modernity: vast, ethnographic museums of alien cultures and peoples who lived in a zone of contemporary noncontemporaneousness that would soon disappear before the homogenizing machine of industrial capitalism. Behind this invention of loss was a powerful desire for an elsewhere, located in the then and there that managed to displace the here and now of modernity which itself was already a misrecognition of the reproduction of capitalist accumulation. What exoticism constructed was the loss of something, an immense nostalgia for an experience that never existed and that was now made to appear prior to its narrative.[5] In this narrative, the old, precapitalist cultures signifying difference and value have been rediscovered precisely in those colonial sites where the violent process of deterritorialization was proceeding unchecked. (Nineteenth-century archaeology was undoubtedly prompted by this desire to penetrate the mystery of temporally lost and spatially distant civilizations.) Moreover, the idea of loss must be grasped within a context that had already privileged exchange value, the ever recurring relativization (and rationalization) of value driving the determination of price and the disappearance of value itself, which usually referred to those qualities that had remained unchanged and unmoved in the evaluation of the true, beautiful, good, and so forth. Exoticism must be seen as an attempt to redress the imbalance between quantity and quality by finding a time and place where the latter still prevailed. It is important to recall that the exotic project was contemporary to all those efforts to addres the question of value by Marx and Nietzsche through Simmel. These efforts sought to find some stable grounding against the onslaught of relativization unleashed by the market and exchange. Ultimately, these concerns with defining value appealed to culture itself, unsurprisingly, as the repository for all subsequent claims of immovable and authentic values capable of anchoring experience within a stable identity in the ever-shifting swell of modernity. This was plainly the task that "exots" (the term used by Segalen to designate an earlier generation) like Loti and Hearn set for themselves. It also explains why these writers were encouraged to repress the colonial world which housed the irreducible remainder of difference — eternal and unchanging value (quality) — and why they so often desired union with the putative other that they had reified as alternatives to the mediocrity of modern life. Hearn tried desperately to become Japanese, much like his British contemporary in Kyoto, Ponseby-Fane, who costumed himself in traditional Japanese garb, mastered arcane and archaic Japanese, wrote about imperial mausoleums which he loved to visit and imagined himself living a Japanese life which, in the late Meiji period, was already an anachronism. Loti, another cultural cross-dresser, is best known for his outrageous impersonations of "natives"; he may very well have prefigured Lawrence's later decision to dress in drag in order to perform as an authentic Arab. With Loti there is an insurmountable yearning for identification with the other—a thinly concealed eroticism which, in the hands of Segalen, becomes a desire for an abstract absolute called the aesthetics of diversity. Yet we must recognize in this fetishistic reunion with the other a discovery of a true self that was not so much a desire to recover a lost identity as it was a crucial and strategic displacement. This strategy of displacement corresponds to exoticism's penchant to repress the historicity that produced the colonial context which constituted the scene of exotic enactment. I am here referring to the displacement of modernity's true other: the industrial worker, whose figure is mapped onto the "native" that inhabits a place that is elsewhere and thus free from—because existing in another temporality and space—the conflict producing uncertainties of class struggle and the division of labor. (This misrecognition of the identity between the industrial worker of Euro-America and the colonized laborer has found its way into postcolonial discourse in all those attempts to psychologize the relationship between colonizer and colonized and locate an alternative modernity born from an anticolonial nationalism derived from uncontaminated native resources.) If, in any case, exots failed to acknowledge an identity between a colonial present and the indeterminate time and place of the other which had become the sublime object of their desire, they also fashioned the native into a figure that embraced all that modernity's real other lacked. Fleeing from the "dangerous and laboring classes," they sought immediate identification with a fictive "native" other, already imbedded in colonized labor, whose activity still echoed the violence of expropriation despite the exoticist effort to repress it by removing the colonial scene from consideration. But what the exots invariably overlooked was that the "native" other, much like the industrial worker, was already being pulled into the vortex of a vast machine of assimilation promoting "imitation" of the kind theorized in Gabriel Tarde's late-nineteenth-century treatise *Les Lois de l'imitation.* Tarde's theory sought to supply a conception of "social tissue" founded on the presumption of lower class imitation of the upper classes as a means to achieve genuine commonality and the guarantee of social solidarity. Yet the fear of social disorder caused by class conflict—addressed earlier by Durkheim—was no less concealed in Tarde's thesis than in the exotic project to displace colonial violence and expropriation by valorizing the native as "other" to capitalism, even though drawn into the productive system. Kipling's short story, "The Man Who Would Be King," reminds us of the misbehavior and disorder caused by the lower classes once they were removed from the industrial city and entered the ranks of the British colonial army to live out the opportunities for fantasy it offered in subjected places like India.

Segalen was sharply dismissive of the earlier generation of exots, calling them "pseudo-Exots . . . the Panderers of the Sensation of Diversity," even though he acknowledged a personal admiration for Kipling and Hearn. "The Lotis," he wrote elsewhere in the text, "are . . . mystically drunk with and unconscious of their object. They confuse it with themselves and passionately intermingle with it, 'drunk with their god!'" They are travelers and mere tourists in space, restlessly visiting one strange place after another before the world runs out of places whose remoteness still offers the promise of mystery, spectators of the spectacle of difference who seek only contrast and comparison and the sensation of having seen lands no (white) man had called upon. Determined to strip the word exoticism of its exclusive and familiar associations with tropicality, vulgar spectatorship, and the regime of geographic adventure, Segalen was persuaded that exoticism was as dependent upon the dimension of time as it was upon space. The earlier exotics had privileged space over temporality in their touristic (and voyeuristic) desire to travel to an elsewhere. In Segalen's rewriting of the space of exoticism, an indeterminate nowhere allows the exoticist to travel in time, in history. By the same measure, Segalen discounted the "colonial, the colonial bureaucrat" who has no other goal but the desire for native trade and commercial relations. Moreover, the bureaucrat's main task is to execute and enforce laws which, accordingly, "render him deaf to the *disharmonies* (or harmonies of Diversity)." Both the colonial and the bureaucrat have failed to reach a level of "aesthetic contemplation." For this reason, Segalen reasoned, colonial literature held no interest for exoticism.

In fact, his conception of exoticism was emptied of considerations of space or place and, as such, the desired elsewhere of the "pseudo-Exots." Although Segalen acknowledged that he had written an essay on exoticism, he advised that it "cannot be about such things as the tropics or coconut trees, the colonies or Negro souls, nor about camels, ships, great waves, scents, spices, or enchanted islands. It cannot be about misunderstandings and native uprisings, nothingness and death, colored tears, oriental thought, and various oddities, nor about any of the preposterous things that the word 'Exoticism' commonly calls to mind." Rather, it is about time — "Going back: history. An escape from the contemptible and petty present. The elsewheres and the bygone days." But, he added, it is also about the future to come. Marked by a recognition of difference, the "perception of Diversity," and the "knowledge that something is other than one's self," exoticism is the act of the conscious being who, in conceiving of himself, can only do so as "*other* than he is." In this revelatory moment of self-discovery, when the conscious individual sees himself in a true light and thus other than what he thought he was, he "rejoices in his Diversity," in the recognition of his difference from others. The other that the individual ultimately finds is in himself and is himself. By bringing otherness back to the present and back to one's place and reinstating its manifestation in the autonomous artist rather than in the wage laborer, now fused to the amorphous figure of the "people," Segalen disclosed a lived history despite — and perhaps because of—the absence of any reference to the circumstances that produced it and the bearers of its tradition. By bringing the mystery once associated with an elsewhere back to one's own time and place, his essay prefigured the later surrealist discovery of the mystery in the everyday.

For Segalen return and self-discovery meant a reunion with one's home. But home was not place but rather a temporality, an "epoch," the "pleasure of living in a particular epoch in relation to others." But such a temporal existence can be realized only by the individual since the experience of exoticism is only "*singular,* individualistic," never associated with "plurality," the masses, or what Heidegger later called "them." It means also freedom from the object that is felt or being described. Unlike earlier exoticists, fixed on and indeed enslaved by the object and racing for identification with it, Segalen confessed that he never desired to be Chinese. Exoticism promised the recovery of an "original purity," which meant rejoining the lost "feeling of experiencing the purity and intensity of Diversity." In its rejection of a tedious, mediocre, and endless present, exoticism in his sense resembled Bovaryism—the quest to escape the banality and boredom of everyday life where yesterday, today, and tomorrow are indistinguishable. What would redeem the banality and conformism of everyday life was art or what he called "creative error," an existence that produced diversity and recognized the need to valorize its different forms. For Segalen, the difference and diversity observed earlier in the colonial scene was now brought back home to "stir" him anew and to put into practice this aesthetic in a life that was already in the process of being flattened and crushed into a shapeless sameness. "If," he warned, "the homogenous prevails in the deepest reality, nothing prevents one from believing in its eventual triumph over sensory reality. . . . The way will be cleared for the Kingdom of the Lukewarm; that moment of viscous mush without inequalities, falls, or reboundings, was prefigured grotesquely by the disappearance of ethnographic diversity."

The earlier exoticists encountered a world that still offered the prospect of an elsewhere uncontaminated by industrial capitalism and thus an escape from the proletarian other to a sanctuary occupied by a native other not yet drawn into the devastatingly disruptive whirlpool of the division of labor. But Segalen was writing on the eve of the Great War and thus from a temporal perspective that already reflected the intense competitive expansion of Euro-America in Africa and Asia. All that was left of the exoticists' dream was an indeterminate elsewhere of difference situated either in the past or the future which only the poet and the dreamer would be able to imagine. These imaginaries of past and future promised to deliver the poet from the present and the incipient regime of mass politics and culture. "There used to be a considerable distance between the Tsar and the muzhik—" Segalen observed, "the Son of Heaven and the people, despite the paternal theory: ancient courts, the small courts of Germany, or the princely cities of Italy were some of Diversity's beautiful tools. The rule of the people brings with it the same customs, the same functions everywhere." With this perception, he was already providing testimony to the emerging shape of mass society and consumer culture where quality and value were vanishing under the weight of quantity and the regime of sameness and mere sensation and where the "mysterious within, the mysterious, which is the quivering approach, the extraordinary scent of Diversity" has been effaced by the war. It is interesting to note that Segalen, who privileged the poetic fragment in his *Essay,* later turned to the novelistic form with the publication of his narrative, *René Leys,* which tried to capture the enormity of China's diversity—its vast otherness and unfathomable mystery. But it was precisely this sense of the mysterious associated with diversity that he brought home on the eve of the war and which became the reconstituted vocation of exoticism. Not too many years later Walter Benjamin, as already suggested, would detect in the everyday at its most ordinary precisely the mystery Segalen had brought back from China but failed to

grasp: the new vocation of the creative artists, that is, difference—the strange, unexpected, surprises—"everything that is
Other." Aesthetics was another word for diversity. Elsewhere,
Segalen worried over the manifest "Wearing Down" of exoticism announced by "everything we call Progress." If Pierre Loti
still lived in a society that offered the ethnographic diversity of
an elsewhere and thus an escape route from the "laws of applied
physics; mechanical modes of travel making people confront
each other," and the horror of intermingling them, "mixing
them up without making them fight each other," it also caused
an undeniable weakening of religion, prompting Segalen to
ask: "where is the mystery?—Where are the distances?"

It was this rewriting of the text of exoticism to underscore
the project of realizing authentic difference that reinforced the
formation of modernism and the autonomy of art as the best de-
fense against the leveling of mass culture and politics. We know
that Segalen's encounter with China's vastness and the stagger-
ing spectacle of its diversity confounded his own capacity to en-
visage the totality.[6] This encounter also supplies an explanation
for the fragmentary, incomplete nature of his essay on exoticism and its privileging of poetry. In his later novel, *René Leys,*
we learn that China's remoteness exceeds the quest's promise
to reach the heart of diversity and the center of mystery itself.
But the essay on exoticism had already brought him back to a
home which, unstable and unfixed even though familiar, would
lead to a doubling consisting of the identification of the singular self with the other and thus to a destabilization of the
subject itself. This was precisely the problem modernism would
undertake to address in the succeeding years between the wars
and in the progressive capitalist transformation of the globe.
While we can locate a genealogical kinship between Roland
Barthes's later *Empire of Signs* and the attenuated nostalgia performed by Simon Leys (Pierre Rycksman) in *Chinese Shadows,*
the sign of an afterlife of the text on exoticism was expressed
first by the Japanese writer Tanizaki Junichiro, who probably

had never read Segalen. A modernist who lived through the accelerated capitalist modernization that Japan witnessed in the interwar period and who faced the prospect of mass culture and the rapid disappearance of difference, Tanizaki exoticized an indeterminate, precapitalist past and its endangered aesthetic endowment to create an exoticism within rather than without and elsewhere. In his melancholic *In'ei raisan* (Praising Shadows), Tanizaki, like other contemporaries, appealed to the difference of Japan's premodern aesthetic sensibility as a figure of radical otherness capable of still haunting and animating the modern self and as a reminder of how modern life was threatening to destroy all diversity. Like Segalen, Tanizaki believed in the necessity of an autonomous art and thus culture as the only fortification against the assault of commodification and the regime of the ever-new in the ever-same because it was the repository of true and unchanging value. Tanizaki's modernist exoticism saw in ancient Japan a timeless aesthetic order based upon the ceaseless play and gradations of light and dark and the production of "shadows" that constituted an optic through which the Japanese grasped their world. Modern machine civilization brought excessive "illumination," both in the shape of "reason's light" and the incandescent light bulb that irradiated everything so sharply that it managed to destroy the subtle and nuanced grades of light and dark—difference—generated by the world of shadows.

The quality that we call beauty, however, must always grow from the realities of life, and our ancestors, forced to live in dark rooms, presently came to discover beauty in shadows, ultimately to guide shadows towards beauty's end. And so it has come to be that the beauty of a Japanese room depends on a variation of shadows, heavy shadows against light shadows—it has nothing else. . . . The hue (of the walls) may differ from room to room but the degree of difference will be ever so slight; not so much a difference in color as in shade, a difference that will seem to exist only

in the mood of the viewer. And from these delicate differences in the hue of the walls, the shadows in each room
take on a tinge peculiarly their own.[7]

What Tanizaki sought to restore with this ironic celebration of a
past that already had passed into the imagination was a reunion
of art and life itself, a program already figured in Segalen's *Essay
on Exoticism.*

But the imprint of Segalen's exoticism is more directly visible
in Roland Barthes's *Empire of Signs* (1970), perhaps its true "after-
image." When Segalen severed exoticism from the specific site
of colonialism and its historic circumstances to explore the un-
steady relationship between self and other that concluded in
inverting the former into the latter, he opened up the way for
subsequent efforts to envision a place of otherness and difference capable of putting into question the claims of the sover-
eign self imagined in the "West." This was undoubtedly the
program pursued by Roland Barthes in his widely read *Empire
of Signs,* which actually carried Segalen's exoticism of nowhere
to a new level of criticism in a time of decolonization (but not
yet postcoloniality). Barthes openly acknowledged an intention
to "imagine a fictive nation" for the purpose of forming a system of features he will call Japan. His interest is in locating the
"possibility of difference" as a condition of beginning the difficult task of writing a "history of our obscurity" and making
manifest the "density of our narcissism."[8] His "dream" is to
"discover certain unsuspected positions of the subject in utter-
ances," and then to imagine writing that is without a subject, a
center, and thus intends no meaning whatsoever. Yet to make
this move Barthes must rethink the otherness of his own cultural endowment, which can only be envisioned in terms of the
claims associated with Western centeredness and subjectivity.

Finally, the echoes of Segalen's exoticism are audible in the
construction of a reverse critique by the sinologist and art historian Simon Leys. Leys, who self-consciously chose the last
name of Segalen's hero René Leys, directed his critique against

the French intellectuals of *Tel Quel* (Barthes, Kristeva, etc.) who, in the 1970s, unashamedly and unblushingly embraced a Maoism pledged to destroy a China he knew and loved. "Exoticism is not dead," writes Leys, who saw in the contemporary voyaging of French intellectuals to Maoist China a replay of Pierre Loti's turn of the century "dreamy Asiatic dilly-dallying."

> Today, if we are to believe a recent article in the *Le Monde,* the aesthetes of *Tel Quel* seem to have found again in China the exquisite secrets of Madame Chrysantheme's patron. We know that the campaign against Confucius and Lin Piao has already caused blood to flow; a friend, an English Sinologist . . . told me the names of the first batch of people executed in this campaign was posted on the walls. . . . But Roland Barthes, confronted with such posters, would no doubt see only calligraphy 'with a grand lyrical movement, elegant and willowy,' and the enigma of those graceful hieroglyphics would not bother him much — now that he has discovered how ridiculous we are when we think that our intellectual talk is always to try to find meaning.[9]

Here, Leys appeals to Lu Xun's earlier observation that Chinese civilization was "nothing but a vaunted banquet of human flesh to be devoured by the rich and powerful" and warned that foreigners who praise the Chinese know nothing. But Lu Xun was also protesting against a particular cultural endowment that behaved "cannibalistically," a kind of prescient anthropophagy Chinese practiced on themselves. For Leys, in any case, this fashionable Maoism was reminiscent of an earlier passion for *chinoiserie* in Europe — a "new exoticism based, like the earlier ones, on ignorance and imagination." In its place, Leys offers precisely the exoticism of the dream world constructed by the Sinologist who, presumably, is in the position to know. His dismissal of Barthes's unknowing admiration for calligraphy already announces the conceit of sinology which, since its beginning, has been based upon an acquisition of Chinese as the primary and necessary condition of grasping the totality of the civilization figured by its writing system. But this world is as much a Western fantasy and dream work of desire as the one it supposes to correct, a timeless, unified cultural domain, founded on a presumed (but never articulated) holism—what Leys calls a "monolithic whole"—that owes more to its Mandarin custodians than it does to "scientific" research. It also runs the risk of being as contemptuous of the Chinese as those intellectuals he wishes to excoriate. Driven by an unconquerable nostalgia for what might have been and fueled by anger provoked by the destruction of the phantasmagoric vision imagined by sinology, Leys's intervention resembles the response of people like Tanizaki who contemplated an aesthetic arcadia in the modern ruins of the twentieth century. It is well to remember that Tanizaki was witnessing and contemplating in the late 1920s the disappearance of the last traces of cultural difference that marked Japanese life before the advent of modernity. Where Leys differed was in writing at a distance—spatial and cultural—from the sublime object of his desire that could only render his own intervention as a form of resentment against history and its challenge to unchanging value. While we can agree with his desire to hold intellectuals accountable to standards of knowledge when they make pronouncements, we must also juxtapose this critique with an impulse that claims for itself the right to have opinions that are neither certified nor fettered by the fetish of specialized expertise and which thus manage to call attention to the spurious and often equally untenable goal of maintaining an ahistorical and exotic fantasy image of cultural value such knowledge is made to serve. Such a move was not only consistent with a certain understanding of Maoism but redolent of Segalen's great program to rethink exoticism by bringing it home. We are indeed fortunate to have this thoughtful translation of Segalen's text on exoticism to remind us once again of this great unfinished project.

Harry Harootunian
New York University

Acknowledgments

My initial research on Segalen was generously supported by the Isaac Walton Killam Postdoctoral Fellowship at Dalhousie University and by the Mary Isabel Sibley/Phi Beta Kappa Postdoctoral Fellowship. Research for this translation and edition of *Essay on Exoticism* was aided by grants from the Queen's University Advisory Research Committee and from Queen's University-SSHRC Research Seed Funding.

For her meticulous and thoughtful comments on the translation, I would like to thank Colette Tonge. Her many corrections and suggestions have been incorporated into the text, resulting in a more accurate and eloquent translation. For supporting this translation project, I thank Fredric Jameson and Reynolds Smith at Duke University Press.

I am indebted to Yvonne Y. Hsieh for her work on Victor Segalen and for her helpful advice, and to Chris Bongie for his invaluable suggestions for the translation project when it was first proposed to Duke University Press. I also wish to thank Michael Bishop and Sima Godfrey for their support at various stages of my research on Segalen.

Without the continual help and encouragement of Glenn Willmott, who was always willing to discuss the thorny problems of translation with me, and who read and commented on my manuscript at various stages with his special care and insight, this project could not have been completed. And finally, for their steadfast support and love, I thank my parents, Haim and Salomeia Schlick.

Introduction

Since its initial publication in 1955, Victor Segalen's *Essay on Exoticism: An Aesthetics of Diversity* has gained increasingly wider acclaim as an important voice in contemporary debates on cultural alterity and has been discussed by such major cultural critics as James Clifford and Tzvetan Todorov.[1] It has also come to serve as a touchstone for postcolonial and Francophone studies, and writers like Edouard Glissant and Abdelkebir Khatibi have seen in the figure of Segalen and in the essay in particular, a critique of conventional exoticism and an attempt to get beyond colonizing attitudes by positing a mechanism for appreciating difference and recognizing difference as an aesthetic value—for being capable, as Segalen writes, of "conceiving otherwise."[2] The use of two quotations from Segalen's essay—one exalting the importance of diversity and difference and the other decrying diversity's decline—in Jean Bernabé, Patrick Chamoiseau, and Raphaël Confiant's manifesto *Eloge de la Créolité/In Praise of Creoleness,* where they appear alongside quotations by Aimé Césaire, Edouard Glissant, and Franz Fanon, attests to a recognition of Segalen's work on exoticism, as well as to his contribution to a contemporary theoretical discourse intent on reconfiguring the relationship between self and other.[3] The essay thus stands as an important link between colonial and postcolonial periods and between colonial and postcolonial critical writing. While contemporary use of Segalen's essay may overlook some of its important historical biases, there is no question that Segalen's desire to reconfigure typically colonialist-exoticist conceptions and to entertain the possibility of a different kind of cultural politics persists as a force to be reckoned with in current debates.

Essay on Exoticism is a crucial document for colonial studies. Though the uncompleted essay is replete with repetitions, internal contradictions, and unsustained assertions, Segalen's intent is nonetheless clear: a desire to critique his contemporaries for their imperialist conceptions of difference and to dissociate himself and his own conception of exoticism from what can more generally be called a romantic-exoticist tradition. This tradition was exemplified for Segalen by the "pseudo-Exot" Pierre Loti, who was popular at the end of the nineteenth century, but stretches back to such earlier nineteenth-century romantic writers as George Sand and Alphonse de Lamartine, who misconstrue the relationship to nature—nature being one type of "exotic" otherness in Segalen's vision—by understanding it merely "as the corollary to their own selves." But if Segalen continually strives to critique narratives of the past, he is no less interested in criticizing his contemporaries: colonial novelists like Marius-Ary Leblond and Emile Nolly, who in his eyes see no problem subsuming the exotic within the colonial, and "impressionistic" travel writers like Jean Ajalbert and Paul Bonnetain, whose work arose alongside the great expansion of France's colonial empire in the late nineteenth and early twentieth centuries. Segalen's attempt to distinguish his understanding of the exotic from theirs is part of his project to strip the very word 'exoticism' of "all its innumerable scoriae, flaws, stains . . . that such continued use by so many mouths, so many prostituting tourist hands have left it with."

Of the other side of the equation, the need to reconstitute and reconfigure an exoticism along different lines, Segalen is keenly aware: if previously colonialist attitudes perverted the capacity to sense out and appreciate the exotic, then an aestheticizing, restorative vision must replace them. If modernity has entailed an acceleration in the means and modes of travel and thereby an unprecedented intermingling of cultures and peoples, and thus a waning of difference, that process has to be resisted by a renewed appreciation for differences or by an ever finer eye and capacity to experience the ever finer differences which remain intact. If exoticism is apprehended and interpreted vulgarly by the large majority of individuals, authority to speak of it must be limited to the great artist, to the individual possessing a strong individuality: the "Exot." If the waning of class, gender, and cultural difference in the world points to the decline of exoticism in absolute terms, its essential nature as part and parcel of the conception of the self (the notion that the self is other to the self, which he derives from Jules de Gaultier's *Le Bovarysme*) has to be recognized and affirmed.

It is important when considering both Segalen's contribution to postcolonial discourse and to colonial theories of exoticism to note that Segalen's use of the word "diversity" (*"le divers"* as he often calls it) does not in itself indicate the kind of intermingling suggested by *métissage* or *créolité*. In the essay, "diversity" does not refer in the first instance to a kind of multiculturalism or to the close coexistence of (cultural, class, or gender) differences. Rather it refers to the existence of absolute (if not essential) differences between peoples and cultures in the world. So that when, for example, Segalen laments the decline of diversity, he is lamenting the breaking down of these differences and their disappearance due to such processes as cultural intermingling, democracy, and feminism. Thus diversity for Segalen is not initially a moral concept; rather, it is an ontological concept to which he accords aesthetic value, as the subtitle of his essay indicates. This is the paradox of Segalen: while current assessments of his writing on exoticism remain aware and critical of his undemocratic remarks regarding feminism and class differences, his frequent elitist stances (e.g., his Nietzschean exaltation of the great man), and his attempt to sidestep historical realities in favor of positing an aesthetics, his work has also been rightly recognized as struggling to forge a new understanding of alterity relevant to postmodernity.

That the essay was never completed is perhaps an indication that Segalen was not able to smooth out the contradictions of his own reconceptualization of exoticism, and it is tempting to ponder what a final version might have looked like. And yet, it is clear from the text we do have that Segalen always intended the essay to have a fragmentary form. As early as 1908 he imagines sending forth his vision "in the form of short, dense, and nonsymbolic prose pieces." Later that same year he imagines his text as "a series of Essays, which, in accordance with this spontaneous 'development' of ideas, will proceed from the idea of Diversity." An *essai* in the French tradition going back to Michel de Montaigne is an attempt, a means of putting forth and testing out one's hypotheses at the very moment that one is making of this test or attempt a textual product called an essay. "This work," writes Segalen in a 1911 entry, "is not an assertion so much as a search. If I undertake to write it, it is not in order to display fully-formed ideas, but in order to help me think this matter through." The answer, he emphasizes, is "not known in advance." Both Segalen's insistence on the essay-nature of his text and our knowledge of his generally intense preoccupation as a modernist writer with questions of literary form should lead us to think of this text not as a series of fragments which have yet to come together in some coherent fashion but rather as something akin to what a final and aphoristic version might have looked like had Segalen, who died at such an early age, been able to complete his work.

Previous Editions

Segalen published only three works in his lifetime: *Les Immémoriaux* in 1907, *Stèles* in 1912, and *Peintures* in 1916. A portion of *Essay on Exoticism* first appeared in 1955 in two installments of the *Mercure de France*. The entries selected for publication were chosen by Pierre Jean Jouve and published as "Notes sur l'exotisme."[4] A complete edition was published as *Essai sur l'exotisme (Notes)* in 1978, more than twenty years later. This text was edited and annotated by Dominique Lelong and introduced by Annie Joly-Segalen. The dated entries were supplemented by portions of Segalen's correspondence which shed light on his exoticism project, and by several lengthy explanatory-biographical notes inserted between the entries to signal time lapses between entries and to explain Segalen's activities at the time of their composition.[5] The subsequent 1986 edition, now titled *Essai sur l'exotisme,* is a reprint of the 1978 edition, but eliminates the explanatory notes within the text in favor of a lengthier introduction by Gilles Manceron. This edition also provides the reader with two essays by Segalen on Paul Gauguin and with his short story "Le Maître du Jouir."[6] The text of *Essai sur l'exotisme* in the collected works of Segalen edited by Henry Bouillier follows the format of the 1986 edition, as does this present translation, but it omits the selections from Segalen's correspondence.[7]

A Note on the Translation

In the interest of providing as faithful a translation as possible, I have reproduced Segalen's capitalization and emphases, although these are somewhat erratic and inconsistent. (For example, words like "Diversity" or "Exoticism" are often, but not always, capitalized.) I have also had to distinguish in this English text between Segalen's frequent use of suspension points (three closely spaced periods), indicating interruptions or breaks in thought, and ellipsis points (three periods separated from each other by a space), indicating missing portions of text.

The language of this text is not always inclusive (using "man" for "humankind") or current (using "native," say, rather than "indigenous"). But I have kept these terms as part and parcel of Segalen's time. For this reason I have also retained the older

Wade-Giles romanization system for Chinese words rather than using the *pinyin* system spellings.

This English edition reproduces the typographic strategy present in both the 1978 and 1986 French editions of *Essai sur l'exotisme,* which distinguishes the letters written by Segalen from his entries on exoticism by italicizing them. Segalen's own notes to his entries appear at the bottom of the page, while explanatory notes are to be found at the end of the text. Those notes which have been translated from the French edition of the work, annotated by Lelong, are indicated as such. Otherwise, the endnotes are my own.

Chronology: Victor Segalen
(1878–1919)

1878   Victor Joseph Ambroise Désiré Segalen is born on 14 January in Brest, his parents' first son. His family is middle class and Catholic. A sister, Jeanne, is born in 1883.

1888   Segalen attends a Jesuit school where discipline is very strict. There he meets Henry Manceron and Max Prat, who are to be his life-long friends.

1893–98   Having passed both his baccalaureate exam and his entrance exam for medical school, Segalen begins his studies at the Ecole de Santé Navale in Bordeaux.

1901   For his thesis, Segalen decides to write about neurotics in contemporary literature. In the course of its preparation in Paris, he meets several important scientists and novelists. Among them are Max Nordau, Huysmans, and Remy de Gourmont, the last of whom introduces him to a circle of writers associated with the *Mercure de France* journal. A portion of his thesis is published in the *Mercure de France* the following year under the title "Les Synesthésies et l'école symboliste."

1902–4   In October, after an internship at the maritime hospital in Toulon, Segalen leaves for Tahiti aboard *La Durance*. Falling ill in San Francisco (where he has the opportunity to visit Chinatown) delays his arrival in Tahiti until 23 January 1903. In Tahiti, Segalen be-

comes interested in the work of Paul Gauguin, who
dies in May 1903. He visits the island of Hiva-Oa in
August, where he meets those who knew Gauguin
and visits Gauguin's house. His article about the artist, "Gauguin dans son dernier décor," is published
in the *Mercure de France* in June 1904. It is during this
year that Segalen first makes note of his desire to
"write a book on exoticism," and his first entry, dated
October 1904, clearly reflects the strong impression
which his experiences in Tahiti, and especially his belated "encounter" with Gauguin, made upon him.
His next entry will not be until June 1908, just prior
to his departure for China.

1905   Due to a stop in Djibouti upon leaving Tahiti for
France in January 1905, Segalen interviews the Rhi-
gas brothers about the writer Arthur Rimbaud whom
they knew, and he subsequently begins a study of
Rimbaud. "Le Double Rimbaud" is published in the
Mercure de France in April 1906. During this time, Segalen is also working on what will be his first published
novel, *Les Immémoriaux*. He arrives back in France on
4 February 1905.

1905–6   During a leave, he meets and courts Yvonne Hébert,
the daughter of a doctor from Brest. They marry in
June. Their first son, Yvon, is born on 15 April 1906.

1906   At this time, Segalen meets two men who will have a
strong influence on him: Claude Debussy, to whom
he proposes a collaboration, and Jules de Gaultier, a
philosopher and author of works on German thinkers
such as Kant, Nietzsche, and Schopenhauer.

1907   "Dans un monde sonore," a story about an individual
who lives solely in a world of sound, appears in the
Mercure de France in August. In September, Segalen's
first major work, *Les Immémoriaux,* is published. It
tells of the decline of Maori civilization as a con-

sequence of its first contact with Europeans in the first half of the nineteenth century. The title of the work refers to those who have forgotten their customs, their gods, and their traditional knowledge — in short, to those who have forgotten their own past by adopting European values and customs. Both of these texts are published under the pseudonym Max Anély.

1908–10   Segalen contemplates an assignment in the Far East, in preparation for which he begins to study Chinese at the Ecole de Langues Orientales in Paris. He leaves for China in 1909 as a student-interpreter. His goal while in China is to improve his Chinese. His arrival in Beijing in June 1909 is quickly followed by a major expedition to central China which he undertakes with his friend Auguste Gilbert de Voisins. Segalen's wife joins him in February 1910, and the family journeys to Beijing via Shanghai, arriving in the Chinese capital at the end of March. As part of a French delegation, Segalen is admitted to see the Emperor. (This visit is transformed into an important episode in the novel *René Leys,* wherein the protagonist is allowed an exceptional peek into the Forbidden City).

1911–12   Segalen moves from Beijing to Tientsin in 1911 to take up a position as professor at the Imperial Medical College. His second child, Annie, is born in August 1912. Segalen's second major work, a collection of prose poems inspired by Chinese steles and titled *Stèles,* is printed in the same month in Beidang. This first edition contains forty-eight poems. Sixteen new prose poems are published in the *Mercure de France* the following year, and these are included in a second, definitive edition of *Stèles,* printed in 1914. *Stèles* is dedicated to Paul Claudel, the author of *Connaissance de l'Est.*

1913–14   In July, Segalen returns to France, where he is successful in raising funds from the French government for an archaeological and topographical expedition in China. A second son, Ronan, is born in November 1913, just as Segalen is beginning preparations for the expedition with Gilbert de Voisins and a naval officer, Jean Lartigue. But the expedition, which begins in February 1914, is soon interrupted by the outbreak of World War I. The three men return to France, where Segalen is assigned to work at the hospital in Brest.

1915–16   After being sent to fight in Belgium in May 1915, Segalen falls ill with acute gastritis and returns to take up administrative duties at the hospital in Brest. *Peintures,* a work whose premise is a narrator's commentary on a series of imaginary Chinese paintings, is published in June 1916.

1917–19   In January 1917, Segalen returns to China as part of a military mission to recruit Chinese laborers for work in French munitions factories. He returns to France in March 1918, taking up his position in Brest after medical training in Paris during May, June, and July. In January 1919 he is hospitalized in the psychiatric ward of the Val-de-Grâce hospital in Paris and subsequently departs for two months of convalescence in Algeria with his wife. On May 21 he leaves for a walk in the woods at Huelgoat, east of Brest. When he does not return, a search party recovers his body, finding evidence of a fatal accident. He had likely fainted from a hemorrhage caused by a deep cut near his ankle and not regained consciousness.

Essay on Exoticism: An Aesthetics of Diversity

Write a book on exoticism. Bernardin de Saint-Pierre—Chateaubriand—Marco Polo, the initiator—Loti.[1]

Include the fewest number of quotations possible.

Argument: Parallelism between stepping back in time (Historicism) and moving out in space (Exoticism).

Study each of the senses and its relation to exoticism: sight, the sky. Hearing: exotic melodies. Smell above all. No taste or touch.

Sexual Exoticism.

Sight. The painters of exoticism. The painter-novelist (Fromentin). Gauguin.[2]

The sensation of exoticism: surprise. Rapidly dulled.

Exoticism is willingly "tropical." Coconut trees and torrid skies.

Not much Arctic exoticism.

Geology. See Pontfilly's book.[3]

9 JUNE 1908.

Counter-impressions—Counter-proofs

From the very heart of the matter.

"I imagined that things were speaking"

It is important that I set down my various views on future exoticism—or even past exoticism—in an orderly series of pages, like prose poems, as clear and as rhythmic as possible.... But consisting of what? Some traveler's "impressions" perhaps? No, not that! Loti already provides these by the score. Saint-Pol, too, would have excelled at this genre had he followed the usual trajectory.[4] And Paul Claudel has done for a small portion of the Far East what, in my youth, I had thought to do for Tahiti: cast a new vision upon it, using a symbolist form. But spontaneously I ended up doing something quite different. And, out of personal necessity, this latter tack must be my point of departure in order to return, as we shall see, to this vision.

So, not Loti, nor Saint-Pol-Roux, nor Claudel.[5] Something else! Something different from what they have done! A true stroke of inspiration *must* be simple... and, to begin, why actually should I not *simply* take the *opposing view* from those views I am defending myself against? Why not strive to *counter*-prove their findings? They expressed what they saw, what they felt in the presence of unexpected *things* and people from which and from whom they sought to experience a shock. Did they reveal what those things and those people themselves thought and what they thought of them? For there is perhaps another shock, from the traveler to the object of his gaze, which rebounds and makes what he sees vibrate. Will not his very intervention—at times so inopportune and venturesome (especially in venerable, quiet, and enclosed spaces)—disturb the equilibrium established centuries ago? Will he not, by reason of his attitude—whether hostile or meditative—arouse mistrust or attraction?... I attempted to express all that, the effect that the traveler has on the living milieu rather than the milieu's effect on the traveler, when I wrote about the Maori race.[6] Here precisely, I am led back to my own preoccupation. Why not do the same thing later to express what I will see: a temple, a Chinese crowd, an opium eater, an ancestral ceremonial, a city of millions of inhabitants... do this for everything that would otherwise become part of a worn exoticism, but which would thereby take on a completely new appearance.

—Yes, no doubt Kipling accomplished this for the Beasts of the Jungle who gaze upon the Little Man and, to some extent, also for the Ship and the Locomotive (though the sense of exoticism was no longer present there).[7] But here my exoticism to the second degree is a matter of stubborn bias, because it is initially obscure and latent and extended outward toward "things," in sum, to the "external world," to the Object in its entirety. This exoticism to the second degree makes up the essential core of my own stance ever since I have systematized it in this way.... In doing so, I will perhaps be able to create a terrain where I feel completely at home, where I will be able to send forth, in the form of short, dense, and nonsymbolic prose pieces the very inverse (so close and so fitting on the front of the page) of my own vision. Upon a ladder of steps made of artifice and skill, would not the highest rung be to express one's vision by an instantaneous, continuous *translation* that would echo one's presence rather than blurt it out bluntly?

Absolute subjectivism, however, is indisputably the only possible metaphysical stance to assume. Any visible transformation has to do only with the method one chooses.... That is to say, the *form* one employs, form being that artificial and miraculous thing that is art's reason for being. So, complete aesthetic justification.

17 AUGUST 1908.

Exoticism

Begin with the *sensation* of Exoticism, at once a solid and elusive ground. Brusquely remove all that is banal from this sensation—coconut trees, camels—and move on to its gorgeous flavor. Do not try to describe it but rather to suggest it to those who are capable of savoring it with rapture....

Then take up what follows... in a series of well-defined Essays. Few quotations. This is not literary criticism.

Then, little by little, extend the notion of Exoticism, like the notion of Bovarysm* (Hindu method),[8] to include:

—the *other sex*. Animals (but not madmen in whom we discover ourselves so well!);

—history. Past or Future. The frantic passing of the Petty Present;

—Everything. Universal Exoticism. The ability to *conceive otherwise.*

Contrast this with the flavor of Individualism. Turn it into a great moving force. A source of nourishment. A vision of beauty.

The Sensation of Exoticism

I

Definition of the prefix *Exo* in the most general sense possible. Everything that lies "outside" the sum total of our current, conscious everyday events, everything that does not belong to our usual "Mental Tonality."

$$\text{So, Exoticism in} \begin{cases} \text{Time} \\ \text{Space} \end{cases}$$

In Time
$$\begin{cases} \text{Past:} & \text{Historical Exoticism, } \textit{chronicles above all.} \\ \text{Present:} & \text{Does not exist by definition.} \\ \text{Future:} & \text{Imaginary Exoticism: Wells, for} \end{cases}$$
example. His mechanism: the dissociation of ideas, and their subsequent reassociation with a peculiar state of mind. Examine the question of "the Future."

---

*The love of other worlds, the world of sound, for example. Strip Exoticism of its "geographic" component.

in $\left\{\begin{array}{l}\text{Maeterlink}^{9}\\ \text{Wells, his prediction of the future.}^{10}\end{array}\right.$

In Space: The only one *I will develop.*

II

Return to the *Sensation of Exoticism.* My whole study of Exoticism will only be concerned with sensations treated as something like irreducible entities. I will therefore examine:

1. The sensation of Exoticism of Space in our era, and in our contemporary minds, according to the following plan:

   a) Etiology. Cause: failure to adapt to the surroundings.

   b) Development. Its ephemeral nature, disappearing with adaptation to the surroundings.

   c) The use it can be put to in:

> *Music*
> *The Plastic Arts*
> *Literature* $\left\{\begin{array}{l}\text{Firsthand}\\ \text{Secondhand}\end{array}\right.$

The disturbances of this sensation. Its absence = Déjà Vu. Its development through the ages — to our own age and beyond.

UPON READING CLAUDEL, 4 OCTOBER 1908.[11]

The position conveyed in this rhythmic, dense, measured, and sonnet-like prose cannot be that of the *I* who feels... but, on the contrary, of the call of the milieu to the traveler, of the Exotic to the Exot[12] who penetrates it, attacks it, reawakens it, *and agitates it.* The familiar *"tu"* will dominate.[13]

This procedure must be measured, almost rhythmic (like a poetic form: ballad or *rondel,* or sonnet — to be determined).

Excerpt from a letter to Max Prat,
written in Paris on 10 December 1908.[14]

I am now renumbering the various facets of my life; which is, alas, more complicated than that of Maître Jacques. 1) Orpheus — take it up again once Debussy has delivered his new symphonic poem, that is, around 20 December.[15] 2) China — of the everyday. 3) A short story about Oceania called La Marche du feu.[16] *I may give it freely to Marius-Ary Leblond. Together with other short stories by Pierre Mille (Africa), Randau (Algeria), Leblond (Madagascar), Nau (the West Indies), and Bertrand (Tunisia), it will make up a book called* Les Exotiques, *which will be published by Calmann-Lévy.[17] As the* Soirées de Médan *did for naturalism, this work will reveal the existence, not so much of a school or a group but of a sincere and fecund exotic moment.[18] Preface — to be examined. I accepted this proposition only for its beneficial effects for my writing and for perfecting my views on exoticism, having initially rebelled against the invitation to submit my story. Despite myself, however, the proposition triggered my imagination and my story emerged in three hours. I will not hold it back in three months' time.*

PARIS, 11 DECEMBER 1908.

Of Exoticism as an Aesthetics of Diversity.
Introduction: The idea of exoticism. Diversity.

Clear the field first of all. Throw overboard everything misused or rancid contained in the word exoticism. Strip it of all its cheap finery: palm tree and camel; tropical helmet; black skins and yellow sun; and, at the same time, get rid of all those who used it with an inane loquaciousness. My study will not be about the Bonnetains or Ajalberts of this world, nor about programs offered by travel agents like Cook, nor about hurried and verbose travelers....[19] What a Herculean task this nauseating sweeping out will be!

Then, strip the word exoticism of its exclusively tropical, exclusively geographic meaning. Exoticism does not only exist in space, but is equally dependent on time.

From there, move rapidly to the task of defining and laying out the sensation of Exoticism, which is nothing other than the notion of difference, the perception of Diversity, the knowledge that something is other than one's self; and Exoticism's power is nothing other than the ability to conceive otherwise.

Having arrived at this progressive contraction of a notion which was so vast in appearance that it seemed initially to include the World and All Worlds; having stripped it of its innumerable scoriae, flaws, stains, fermenting organisms, and molds that such continued use by so many mouths, so many prostituting tourist hands have left it with; having at last taken hold of this notion with a state of mind that is both clear and alive, let us give it the opportunity to restore its solidity, and to develop freely and joyously without hindrance and yet without excessive encouragement, like a purified seed; it will seize all the sensory and intelligible riches that it meets in its process of growth, and, being filled with all these riches, it will revitalize and beautify everything.

This play of thought is no other than the kind of thinking freely to infinity of Hindu thought. The Hindus think, and immediately a particular principle tends to become a universal (see Oldenberg. *Le Bouddha*).[20]

(For fear of betraying myself, this essay must leave no gaps and must forget nothing. I should not be content with "provoking thought," as Montesquieu puts it in reverse.[21] I must exhaust my subject so that nothing else can be said about the sensation of Diversity which does not already exist in potential form here.

Right away, metaphysical analogies present themselves and must be classified, incorporated, or discarded: Schopenhauer's law of Representation that every object presupposes a subject. Jules de Gaultier's law of Bovarysm, that every being which conceives of itself necessarily conceives itself to be other than it actually is.[22] Can it be a question of law here? Here is a fact: I conceive otherwise, and, immediately, the vision is enticing. All of exoticism lies herein.)

Quinton told me that all truth can be found in nature, that in nature we will find that truth which we possess in ourselves.[23] Darwin, an Englishman, discovered a truth of Struggle and Strain. Quinton, a Frenchman, is now moving despite himself toward the idea of a moral instinct.

Now, there are born travelers or *exots* in the world. They are the ones who will recognize, beneath the cold and dry veneer of words and phrases, those unforgettable transports which arise from the kind of moments I have been speaking of: the moment of Exoticism. Without contravening the two aforementioned and formidable laws, which constrain the universal being, exots will attest to the fact that this notion which we have put forth puts the very flavor of the interplay of these laws into relief: the rapture of the subject conceiving its object, recognizing its own difference from itself, sensing Diversity. And, surely, nothing more will be created. But I hope that for them the flavor will be greater and more deeply rooted than before, and that the freedom of this interplay will be beyond measure. It is for them that I write.

Then will follow a series of Essays, which, in accordance with this spontaneous "development" of ideas, will proceed from the idea of Diversity.

I
Individualism

Only those who have a strong individuality can sense Difference.

In accordance with the law which says that every thinking subject presupposes an object, we must assert that the notion of Difference immediately implies a personal point of departure.

Only those with a strong individuality can fully appreciate the wonderful sensation of feeling both what they are and what they are not.

Exoticism is therefore not that kaleidoscopic vision of the

tourist or of the mediocre spectator, but the forceful and curious reaction to a shock felt by someone of strong individuality in response to some object whose distance from oneself he alone can perceive and savor. (The sensations of Exoticism and Individualism are *complementary*).

Exoticism is therefore not an adaptation to something; it is not the perfect comprehension of something outside one's self that one has managed to embrace fully, but the keen and immediate perception of an eternal incomprehensibility.

Let us proceed from this admission of impenetrability. Let us not flatter ourselves for assimilating the customs, races, nations, and others who differ from us. On the contrary, let us rejoice in our inability ever to do so, for we thus retain the eternal pleasure of sensing Diversity. (This may lead to the following question: if we increase our ability to perceive Diversity, will we enrich or impoverish ourselves? Will this rob us of something or endow us with something greater? The answer is clear: it will infinitely enrich us with the whole Universe. Clouard expressed this well when he said: "One can see that this naturalism implies neither our debasement nor dispersion, nor nature's superiority at the expense of human personality. It represents the growing influence of our minds upon the world.")[24]

II
The Exoticism of Nature

And this is our first experience of exoticism. The external world is that which immediately differentiates itself from us. Let us not dwell on those old debates regarding the reality of things. Oh! What does it matter! if they rouse us? For the feeling for nature only *came into existence* when man began to conceive of nature as different from himself.

For a long time man animated nature with his own breath. He ascribed his own passions and gestures to it. Can we say that the Vedas truly grasped nature?[25] No! They animated nature according to the interplay of their own desires. We know to what extent the Greeks ignored nature. We pretend that savages largely ignored it. The sense of a non-anthropomorphic nature, of a nature that is blind, eternal, and immense, a nature that is not superhuman but ex-human and from which all humanity— strangely!—is derived—this sense of nature's exoticism only emerged from the understanding of the forces and laws of nature. These were so remote from human laws and forces that man ran, distraught, to the other end of the world, where he recognized two worlds: the physical world, and the mental world.

III
The Exoticism of Plants and Animals

The distance here is not as great. The flavor is fainter, but the quality of the sensation is more oblique and disquieting. (And all the more disquieting because it is closer to us in the scale of things. A rock is never alarming unless it begins to move or becomes animated. A tree is only frightening when it plays at being a ghost.)

IV
The Exoticism of Human Kinds

This exoticism is almost of a similar nature, though literarily it is the only one which is recognized. (Let us immediately abandon the illusory difference between sages and madmen. There is no Exoticism in considering those deprived of their reason: we discover ourselves so well in them!)

Its innumerable prostitutions.

Its various stages: the "Travel Account," the "Traveler's Impressions."

V

At another level: the direct representation of exotic material as conveyed through form (see project of exotic prose).

VI
The Impenetrability of Races

This is nothing other than the extension of the impenetrability of Individuals to the impenetrability of races.

The treason of language and of languages.

VII
The Exoticism of Moralities

Moral shocks. The great dramas and beautiful agonies of races which ensue from this.

VIII

Of the perfecting of Travel and of the threats to the survival of the flavor of exoticism which follow from Travel.

Thus understood as an integral part of the play of human intelligence, the sensation of Diversity has nothing to fear from the likes of Cook Travel Agencies, ocean liners, airplanes....

Perhaps some balance will be established whereby the constant intermingling of individuals will be redeemed by the small number of individuals who will retain the capacity to feel Diversity. (See Louis Bertrand's article in the *Revue des Deux Mondes*.)[26]

IX
The Exoticism of Race

Extra-terrestrial Exoticism.

The Worlds of Martians and others.

[In the margin] Exoticism of the sexes. This is where all Difference, all incompatibility, all Distance rise up, call for recognition, roar, cry, and weep with either love or frustration. This is akin to the madness Lovers feel when they desire, through some miraculous force, to merge with each other in a way that is as excessive as the Yogi's desire to merge with the Brahma.

X

Para-sensory Exoticism: that is to say, the creation of a world different from our own by its selection of a particular sense as the predominant one (a sonorous world,[27] an olfactory world, etc.) or by its differing Spatial properties: four-dimensional Space.

XI

The Exoticism in Time. Going back: history. An escape from the contemptible and petty present. The elsewheres and the bygone days.

XII

The future to come.

XIII

Finally, the chosen notion and mode of seeing the world which surrounds us, the subject's attitude toward the object having more than fully embraced all thought, the conscious being (by way of the Hindu mechanism) finds himself face to face with his own self.

(After discussing universal Exoticism, we arrive at an essential Exoticism. I am obviously proceeding straight from Jules de Gaultier's thought.)

But even then, the conscious being knows that in conceiving

of himself he cannot but conceive of himself as *other* than he is.
— And he rejoices in his Diversity.[28]

Excerpt from a letter to Max Prat,
written in Paris on 23 December 1908.

*A happy result of my friendship with Debussy is my friendship with
Laloy (of the* Mercure Musical*).[29] Along with yours, I find Laloy's sensibility the most harmonious to my own that I have ever encountered (without changing sex). Our conversations cannot be discussions but, rather, the
alternating expression of our similarities. I would so much like to bring
the two of you together. It so happens that we have almost everything in
common, including the Chinese language, nearsightedness (he exaggerates
his own), respect for opium, and many other things. Moreover, I place him
among those whom I call* EXOTS, *a word I would like to establish in my
dreamed of and already well-defined Essay.* An Exot is a born Traveler,
someone who senses all the flavor of diversity in worlds filled with wondrous
diversities. When you arrive, my unlucky friend, a two-hour lecture on the
subject awaits you! But before that I have something more concrete on my
shelf: my short story (which will not be called* La Marche du Feu*). So
far, it does not repeat the material of* Les Immémoriaux *or encroach
upon* Le Maître du Jouir....

. . . *For China, though consuming, will not make of me its specialist,
I hope. Or even so and above all, Oceania will always provide me with
that immediate and palpable pleasure which refreshes the mind-withering
intellectuality.*

*And if I have something to say which has never been said before, I feel
more and more that it is that very thing into which I have naively plunged
myself: the overpowering flavor of diversity. The very incomprehension people
have of Orpheus is but an instance of the eternal drama of exoticism.*

---

* MAX ANÉLY, "Essai sur l'exotisme": *Une Esthétique du Divers.* Paris, 1918, published
by... 3,50F per volume.[30]

(As to my project, which entails the absorption of the universe by a nascent idea that is gradually growing larger....)

"The wise man . . . recognizes that he almost took a particular liking for something as a principle of certainty, and that in the space of an instant he has conceived *his desire as the center of the universe;* he is all too aware of the passionate origin of the theory which has overwhelmed him. This is how he recognizes its relativity . . . he knows the precise place where this theory has broken the chain of causality to attain his support by leaning on his will. . . ."[31]

(But as for me, my particular aptitude is the ability to sense diversity, which I strive to erect as an aesthetic principle deriving from my knowledge of the world. I know where it comes from — from within myself. I know that it is no more valid than any other principle, but also that it is no less valid.[32] I believe only that I am that individual whose duty it is to bring it to light, and that in doing so I will have fulfilled my mission. "See the world, then put forth one's vision of the world."[33] I have seen the world in its diversity. In turn, I wished to make others experience its flavor.)

24 DECEMBER 1908.

After the essential Exoticism between object and subject comes the Exoticism between the physical world and the mental world.

"Following Taine, we can distinguish and oppose these two worlds to each other; these worlds *appear* to be in a relationship of cause and effect to each other, but it seems impossible to discern their meeting point or mode of communication, so that we must assume that they are irreducible. We have, on the one hand, the mental world that is immediately and interiorly given to us by our consciousness; it includes all mental events, sensations, images, ideas. On the other hand, we have the physiological and physical world, which ends where the other begins. This latter world is only given to us indirectly, through the mediation of the mental world, by means of perception and of the senses. This world is exterior to us. It includes a series of phenomena that occasion the awakening of the mental world. These phenomena are vibratory . . . nerves . . . centers. . . . After that, the setting suddenly changes: the physiological world vanishes and the mental world erupts onto the scene of consciousness with its retinue of images and ideas. For although every molecular movement in our nerve centers is accompanied by a state of consciousness, and although every image presupposes a molecular movement, we do not recognize any connection between a movement and a sensation. They are phenomena of an entirely different order to us. Closer to this notion and to the perspective of ancient metaphysics, we continue to recognize only our sensations in the world we inhabit and remain unaware of the possible resemblance which may exist between our sensations and those external objects whose movements in our nerve centers is their last expression."[34]

Excerpt from a letter to Jules de Gaultier, written in Paris on 28 December 1908.

I have certainly not let a day go by since our last meeting without thinking of you deeply and sometimes even benefiting greatly—in that form which I most value, that is, accomplished work—from your own writing with which I have become more and more permeated. Just as I was getting ready to return those precious pages of the Revue Blanche *to you, I was seized by a final fear of letting such support escape, and so reread them with my now four-year-old, yet still thriving, project in mind: it is to be An Essay on Exoticism, An Aesthetics of Diversity.*

It would be difficult for me to write to you about it. I would hardly risk mentioning it now if I were not to have the very great pleasure of seeing you again in Paris at the end of February. My most serious and strenuous examination of my own thinking has led me to accept only the Hindus and you as the true masters, and then to proclaim this openly. Nietzsche was immensely invigorating for me, but I am not capable of thinking like him. Kant was superb — the early Kant — but I cannot feel the way he does. The Hindus, however, have taught me through play, through the wheels, and through an "expansive" way of thinking that has imposed itself upon me, to let the mind live and expand, and you yourself taught me to direct it. All this relates to Diversity.

Having experienced Exoticism intensely, having experienced all the different types of Exoticism, in Space (races, sexes), and in Time (love of the Past)... and this in an initially completely naive manner, I asked myself what the common element to all those wonderful sensations was. And I think that I have found it, that I have been able to sniff it out: Diversity. It will be my point of departure.

I will then allow it to germinate; and, like the Hindus, I will allow it to absorb everything which surrounds it. But I do not dare summarize this hasty plan to you.... I hope to reach, without a hitch and by another route, the aphorisms which are the only means of shedding light upon the still chaotic path of my thoughts: "The mind . . . experiences a plenary joy in witnessing the birth of an idea, in seeing the diversity of forms and of things rise from some unfathomable abyss of unity."

Or elsewhere: "The transformation brought upon the thing in itself by the mirror of the intellect, seems to be its change from unity to diversity." "Unity can only represent itself to itself through diversity."[35]

So I am going to reread your entire work again. It has, in any event, been with me in its entirety in Paris and will follow me to China; from there, I will go back to Kant; my reading of his work in the course of this year had not been with "the idea of Diversity in mind"; I will then return to you via Schopenhauer. Is this acceptable? And since I ask you for such specific advice, would you let me know (this has to do with pedagogy) which you consider the best translations of The Critique of Pure Reason *and of* The World as Will and Representation? *To date, I have only read various translations haphazardly, that is, depending on copies which various libraries possess.*

Perhaps I seem to you a heretical disciple or an unfaithful one in the development of my ideas, a disciple who is wandering off the path or sinking down into the mud. I can only assert my intellectual indebtedness to you for getting me started. Even if I do not reach my destination, I will have at least set out and lived with this beautiful hope for several years. This hope is entirely thanks to you.

Orpheus, who preoccupied me greatly at the beginning of my stay here in Paris, has taken a happier turn. Debussy's assiduous collaboration frees me from that obsessive literary fear in a reverse sense: I feared "writing" too much, and now I see that the day is not far when my work will result in a prose which remains ductile for his purposes.

As for other matters, my study of Chinese, undertaken with the most lucid of teachers, is not out of keeping with my interest in exoticism, as the study of Chinese surely represents a world of thought that is as poles apart from my own as I could wish.

PARIS, DECEMBER 1908.

My ability to sense Diversity and to recognize its beauty has led me to hate all those who have tried to weaken it (through ideas or forms) or to deny it by constructing tedious syntheses. The Schurés, Péladan at times, the theosophists always, and many occultists....[36]

Others, pseudo-Exots (the Lotis, tourists, had an effect that was no less disastrous. I call them the Panderers of the Sensation of Diversity).

DECEMBER 1908.

Antinomy between: the diversity of human races or the exoticism of races, and the law of intellectual constancy.[37]

2 JANUARY 1909.

Refrain from quoting when providing concrete examples, especially from writers. Admittedly, it is convenient to borrow images or support from those who were the great masters of words when formulating one's thoughts in words. But it would mean falling into the same mistake as a writer who only writes about the artist's soul or the painter who only paints scenes of artists' studios.

Excerpt from a letter to Jeanne Perdriel-Vaissière,[38] written in Paris on 7 January 1909.

Have you seen the wonderful study by Mr. Clouard on Maurice de Gué-rin in the last issue of the Mercure?[39] *He says in his words what I will have to express with my own in an Essay I am writing, where, in the course of several years to come, I will attempt to define the Aesthetics of Diversity, the beauty of exoticism (in its most general sense). Given my own stance, I have to rename what he calls a feeling for nature, but the outcome will be the same as his, above all because of my great admiration for him.*

JANUARY OR FEBRUARY 1909.[40]

The Exoticism of Nature

I must make a distinction between the feeling for nature (which "only came into existence when man began to conceive of nature as different from himself")[41] and the Exoticism of the "External World" (which it may be important to sort out in the earlier chapter, so that it will not repeat what I say in this chapter and in the last chapter on Object and Subject).

Introduction to this chapter

In short, I am returning to that eternal essay on the "feeling for Nature." Its very banality will be the touchstone upon which will be etched or not etched, imprinted or not imprinted, the purity, the originality of my vision. If it sheds light on that insipid jumble of ideas scattered about by the likes of Rousseau, George Sand, and others, it will be because my vision really possesses some special virtue.[42] It does not displease me to impose it upon such mediocre subjects.

But if nothing unexpected comes of all this... let the readers shut the book. It will be because the feeling of Diversity is not in me... or because they did not know how to receive it.

There is an odd opposition between the feeling for Nature and Life in Nature. We do not see, feel, or taste nature with great aesthetic joy until we have experienced a separation or a difference from it. This takes on a remarkable meaning if I follow the play of my thoughts and replace the word "feeling" by the word "Exoticism": the Exoticism of Nature, which can exist only once we feel its difference from ourselves.[43]

In "Maurice de Guérin et le sentiment de la nature," Henri Clouard observes the following:* *"One has often called attention to the belated appearance* of an awareness of and a passion for nature in the soul of civilizations. Without researching here the profound reasons for this phenomenon, and not wishing to concern myself with anything but the *literary aspect* of this question (well said), it must be said that all great aesthetic periods of human history have only preoccupied themselves with what is, strictly speaking, Human. At the edges and neglected at the time lies that life of nature which French literature — as slow as its ancient mothers in this respect — only took up as a subject matter of the first order and equal to the greatest, in the fourth of its great centuries."** [44]

(Clouard successfully highlights what differentiates Maurice de Guérin's ideas from Classicism and Romanticism. A Classicist, de Guérin examines Romanticism's favorite subject.) "Whereas, here is an author of the same period, who remains faithful to the grand and essential lineage of our national literature, and even adds a link to Western Classicism, while making

*For a long time man has animated nature with his own breath. He lent it his passions and his gestures. Can we say the Vedas felt nature? No!
** *Mercure de France,* 1 January 1909.

the passionate feeling for nature the dominant and independent object of his literary efforts."

Maurice de Guérin is a fine example for the Exoticism of Nature of what I plan to do for the Exoticism of Races and Customs: first, immerse myself in them, then extricate myself from them in order to maintain their *objective* flavor (how these same words assert themselves with the same force! I have to arrive at an essential exoticism: that of the *Object* for the subject!). Similarly, Maurice de Guérin first gained a complete understanding of Nature, then completely retreated from it.[45] His Romantic contemporaries, meanwhile, "only understood nature as the corollary to their own selves, and described only some of its particular features." So it is with the Lotis and all "impressionistic tourists."

Maurice de Guérin, therefore, did for the Exoticism of Nature *precisely* what I tried to do for the Exoticism of races in *Les Immémoriaux,* while Chateaubriand (nature and race), Victor Hugo (nature), and Sand! (Nature!) only diluted their object in a mixture in which that wondrous and flavorful Diversity vanished![46]

There are even correlations in our renderings: the story is related by a centaur and "in a centaur-like manner" (in a Maori-like manner).[47] Just as Térii speaks with sorrow of "those pale men and their ridiculous hands," so the centaur despises man... "the centaur, driven out by the gods and reduced by them to the state of crawling around in this way." Herein, exactly, lies the "exotic jolt" which overturns human values!

Clouard expressed this wonderfully: "If Hugo . . . wanted to rise and possess some of the great Pan's qualities, he only got as far as a chaotic pomposity. As for Lamartine, who never created a completed image in the process of composing his lengthy descriptions, nature is nothing but a pretext: a premonition of God. . . ."[48] (Yet others saw . . . only "fragments of souls" which floated up to the surface of the earth, scattered. . . .)[49] Finally, Chateaubriand, having wedded Rousseau's lyrical descriptions to the pictorial descriptions of Bernardin de Saint-Pierre, animates and humanizes very beautiful landscapes. He even steps back so that these landscapes can detach themselves from him, unfurl freely, and exist in and for themselves: the great Being begins to gather his dispersed forces, and reminds one of those grand figures of André Chénier (the eternal oceans bubbling with life)....[50] But de Guérin expressed Nature in its totality and in its fullness. He discovered the breath of the universal being, the mysterious life of a gigantic organism, an absolute and definitive fact, a supreme divinity, which only the writings of Goethe, here and there, have brought to light before.[51]

I would like everything that Clouard says about the feeling (of Exoticism) for Nature in the work of Maurice de Guérin to be said of my own efforts in defining an exoticism of Races! The parallel continues:

"It (nature) is too beautiful, however, and he himself is too passionate not to be tormented by her mysteriousness, in spite of their quite veritably fulfilling unions.[52] In the presence of the loved one, does not the lover despair of all those moments which never were his, but *especially of the utterly irreducible difference which exists between two beings?*" (Cf. "two lovers... " of *Double Rimbaud*.)[53] Is this assertion indeed so widespread?

"Chateaubriand, Senancour, or Amiel—those *Narcissi* of the literary world—have minutely chronicled the subtleties of their own selves.[54] In contrast, the Centaur presents itself to us as an objective, autonomous creation. This little evocative poem has the strength of a bronze" (this is almost word-for-word the way I described my own prose as I wished it to be: "made of bronze: hard and polished").

"While quite different from Jean-Jacques, Werther, Senancour, and René, de Guérin remains nevertheless on the same plane. He created a simple and complete synthesis* of their never-ending *analyses*." (Just before reading this, I was actually thinking that my own concept of exoticism is somewhat related

---

*"My love of nature is not fixated on details but on the totality of those things which exist." Maurice de Guérin, *Journal*.[55]

to a "synthetist" painting, whereas the art of Loti evokes instead those brief *analyses* of the *impressionists.*)

(I must copy what Clouard writes after this! All in all, his essay at once robs me of something yet fills me with joy: for he provides me with an admirable example of the Exoticism of Nature, and treats it in such a way that I will have to give my all in order to outdo him. I must, in any event, seriously take up this matter from the point of view of exoticism.)

"Here is his (Maurice de Guérin's) great distinguishing feature: objectivity. For this objectivity increases any emotion through the firm, solid, eternal quality it bestows upon its object. . . . Maurice de Guérin has simply allied (I have said, with Jules de Gaultier: the compromise of Life, and I believed my aesthetic formula to be no more or less true than any other) the profound feeling of universal Unity and the feeling of the *differences between things.* He has, alternately, made the gods the perfect representatives of harmony and the shadowy figures of mystery. Things remain too distinct and irreducible in his poem for one to discern the ephemeral forms of a unique and eternal being. Yet, in truth, these things that are linked together within the immensity of time and space create such a magnificent and orderly choir that one might say they are orchestrated by the hand of a hidden god. This is precisely what the alleged pantheism of Maurice de Guérin must be limited to!"[56]

It may be that *freedom* is one of the characteristics of the *Exot,* that is, *being free* with regards to the object that is felt or described, at least at that final phase when the Exot has moved away from the object. The Lotis are, quite the contrary, mystically drunk with and unconscious of their object. They confuse it with themselves and passionately intermingle with it, "drunk with their god!" Whereas Clouard writes: "The very force of such beauty will prove, I believe, that it would not have been born without the author possessing complete *freedom* toward his object, or without an incomparably steadfast mind: one must comprehend the thoughtful and purposeful qualities such originality possesses even in its most excited state."

And here is again something I would like people to say about *Les Immémoriaux,* replacing the word "Nature" with the words "Maori race":

"If one admires the rhythm of his sentences, it must be noted that this rhythm is the just reward of a submission to nature understood in all its plenitude. Each sentence wants to evoke what has been called an appearance, an attitude, an action in that it contributes to this plenitude, or, at the very least, signals to what extent this plenitude remains unexpressed."

13 JANUARY 1909.

Sweep away: the colonial, the colonial bureaucrat.

They are nothing like Exots! The former comes into being with the desire for native trade relations of the most commercial kind. For the colonial, Diversity exists only in so far as it provides him with the means of duping others. As for the colonial bureaucrat, the very notion of a centralized administration and of laws for the good of everyone, which he *must* enforce, immediately distorts his judgment and renders him deaf to the *disharmonies* (or harmonies of Diversity). Neither of these figures can boast a sense of aesthetic contemplation.

For this very reason, "colonial" literature is of no interest to us.

Yet, paradoxically, this very sentiment comes from reading the works of enthusiastic "colonizers," like the Leblonds. (*L'Oued.*)[57]

(I believe they extol the virtues of what they refer to as the politics of associationism.[58])

21 FEBRUARY 1909.

The differentiation of the various art forms from each other: what belongs to music, to painting, etc., the opposite of synesthesias. The Palinode.

Palinode of my synesthesias.[59]

I will not allow myself to make any comparison between the
arts for a time. I will not try to justify the nonstylizing realism of Mussorgsky with the indispensable stylization and the
contempt of pictorial realism.

Yes or No? I must think about it. Perhaps, a provisional, pru-
dent attitude.

7 MARCH 1909. CHERBOURG.

The Exoticism of the sexes.

Two oppositions: the frantic search for a mystical purity by
way of Huysmanian vice, and of vice by way of an imagined
purity.[60] Are these not two examples of the play of opposites?
Those who transformed the act of the flesh into a hygienic act
lost everything in doing so; all they gained was that peaceful
homogeneity in which the flavor of Diversity dies out.

(The illogicality of Lafcadio Hearn,* who, following the example of ants, has conjured up a humanity that would limit
sexual functions and, hence, produce a line of long-living neu-
ter beings. But he is a Christian: "The loftiest force is obviously
the force that springs forth from selflessness.")

23 MARCH 1909.

Even in philosophy, the *subject* and the meaning of ideas are
less important than the way they are linked, than the elegance
with which they are set into motion and developed, in short,
than their *play.* What is properly philosophical is only the *play of
ideas,* just as what is profoundly pictorial is the splendor of lines
and colors. The interweaving of ideas in the field of philosophy

---

*Lafcadio Hearn. A better Exot than I would have thought. Son of an Irish father
(doctor in the West Indies) and a Greek mother. Dublin, New York (poverty), New
Orleans, Martinique, Philadelphia, Japan. See article by Mr. Logé in the *Mercure,*
1 December 1909.[61]

is equivalent to the mixing that is essential to the creation of orchestral or pictorial compositions.

23 MARCH 1909.[62]

In order to balance my point of view, which voluntarily claims all my energy, I rely on the existence, out there, of opposing ideas — or what is similar — on those who will exploit them! But it is important not to become encumbered by one's own adversaries if one wishes to dedicate oneself fully to striking out against the insipidness of the real, and to have no caution in the enthusiastic spreading of ideas. . . .

24 NOVEMBER 1909. PI K'EOU.

Miscellaneous notes.

The child's sense of Exoticism. For the child, exoticism comes into being at the same time as the external world. Gradation: at first, everything the child's arms cannot reach is exotic for him. The exotic mingles with the mysterious. From the moment he leaves the cradle, exoticism extends itself to what is within his four walls. As he comes out, a drastic change, he retreats. He integrates his feeling for other places into his experience of his own place; he lives fiercely in that vast world made up of a single house. Whatever he wants is exotic for him. Another abrupt change: as he reads a story, he suddenly realizes that *he will someday be able to experience the very things he is now reading about!* His games go on exactly as before. The game is the same. His state of mind is different. An unknown feeling: desire, a man's emotion. He knows it is a game. But he perpetuates it in his desire to experience it. This is a school of life. This state will last until, one day, he will again begin to put things into question, when he will have to relearn these things in books (history and geography), at which point their exoticism will be dried up and sterilized.

Exoticism in French literature. Very rich. Necessary because the French do not invent. (Corneille: Spaniards. La Fontaine: Aesop and popular storytellers.[63] Gilbert de Voisins[64]: Breithart, Stevenson for his Adventures,[65] *Alice's Adventures in Wonderland* and *Through the Looking-Glass* for the fantastic.)

Exoticism can only be *singular,* individualistic. It does not allow for plurality. One can imagine that an impression of goodness felt by one man can be shared by five hundred; one cannot conceive of a plural exoticism. The buffoons of exoticism thought this was possible! Exoticism is distressing in social art. All the arts partake of universality. The Renaissance was marvelous in France, in Italy, in Holland.... But exoticism in social art is not possible. The English eighteenth century was wonderful for Montesquieu and Mirabeau as individuals, but terrible for France. This is what had given rise to the Roman Empire. Social exoticism brings good fortune for particular individuals and disastrous results for nations. Or, if not disasters, the result is completely contrary to this exoticism. (Augusto compares the similarity between this development and bovarysm, using more or less the same examples.)[66]

28 APRIL 1910.

Essays toward an "Essay on Exoticism"

The Roaming Herds
(in a style that is part sheep pen, part stud farm, part farmland)

If only they were wild! But no; they are the sweetest-tempered among animals, the easiest to handle, to muzzle, to castrate. And if at times they suddenly start up? (of little importance.... The *damages* are material ones....) —Their *ancestors?* How degenerate. Are these the daring travelers, who, abruptly, and by abrupt changes, degenerated from explorers into tourists...? But not at all! They have nothing in common! They have "migrated" in the face of civilization, as is politely said of the expectations of animals now extinct.... The former have turned to doing something else, or something further on or something better. Their ancestors? Simply the homebodies of another time. And in the midst of their worst scurries and wanderings, they return to their nest eggs, their savings, their easy chairs, their siestas. But let us not try to hide it any longer, we are talking about tourists here and ways in which we can protect ourselves from them.

— Their habits. Their customs.

— The changes they bring about in their wake. The damages they cause. Their leavings. The defensive measures taken against them (Nanking), yet more formidable....[67]

— Study them especially *in China*. What they see of China, of the river, of the mountains. What a journalist long ago saw of the penal colony: the walls.

Add to them the False Explorers.

Seeing what they are like, and what they ruin, one might well be very fearful of them from the point of view of a pure exoticism. This issue is worth exploring. I will take up the definition of exoticism. The herds of tourists by the thousands. Americans. The Belgian mission, which spends 22,000 dollars in fifteen minutes, that is, 40 francs per second (this is henceforth how "good taste" will be evaluated). But I must not be discouraged: Exoticism and true exots are not at stake in all this! Let us not forget that the same false excitement was shared by painters in former times: the photograph, then the color photograph. Mechanism and human sensitivity. Only the first may change; the second is immutable. And if tourism does in fact diminish the exoticism of countries, it is because this exoticism took a coarser and more accommodating form. It can be left to tourists as their pasture, while true exots can take refuge on more glacial peaks.

27 MAY 1910.

Exoticism. For the conclusion.

Study the Ming dynasty. Talk about how, a little before becoming "excessively Chinese," the Chinese attained the most generally applicable beauty.[68] This is because diversity for some is a specific kind of nourishment for beauty, but, at the same time and to a certain degree, diversity merges and subsides within something which is no longer different or homogenous but: Beautiful. A kind of palinode for the whole book.

The aesthetic principle is more general than the principle of the aesthetics of Diversity. For example: Ming art is more generally beautiful than K'ang-hi art because it uses less porcelain and is less Chinese.[69] Beauty has generalizing elements which appear to obliterate the Beauty of Diversity—which would then be merely material for beauty, not the realization of beauty.

21 OCTOBER 1910.

Quality and quantity.

In the preface to his poetry collection *Le Royaume de la Terre,* Henri Bouvelet asserts that difference in quality cannot be reduced to difference in quantity.[70] This muddled idea about a total homogeneity seems to me either heretical or impotent in the Kingdom of ideas.

1911.[71]

Far from stifling it, the sensation of Exoticism enhances and enriches one's personality.

The capacity to discriminate is formed through the experience of diversity. Those who are capable of tasting it are strengthened, enhanced, and intensified by the experience. It crushes the others. If it destroys their personality as well, it is because their personality was very weak or made of something other than the true capacity to experience exoticism.

The exot, from the depths of his own clump of patriarchal soil, calls to, desires, sniffs out these beyonds. But in inhabiting them, in enclosing them, embracing them, savoring them, the Clump of earth, the Soil, suddenly and powerfully becomes Diverse. This double-edged balancing game results in an unflagging, inexhaustible diversity. ("Advice to the Discerning Traveler").[72] A wonderful example is that of Jules Boissière, a Provençal and a *félibre,* who wrote his most beautiful lines of verse in the Provençal tongue while in Hanoi.[73] The dying Gauguin painted that pale pink, Brittany church tower in the snow. Boissière allowed that beautiful fruit of Provence to ripen in the tropics. Added riches, mixed together, yet well-ordered. The ridiculousness of individuals belonging exclusively to their *native soil;* —and of those who believe that nothing can be assimilated by us. Well, let us acknowledge the following: even if we did not find maternal nourishment elsewhere than in our native soil, would we not find poison or juices there? Is everything we drink or breathe in destined to turn into bone and muscle? Let us not forget the interplay of ideas. In fact, the sources of nourishment are everywhere around us. What are most often missing are the true appetites to seek them out.

Having long desired to depart, Boissière, once departing, aboard his ship headed for Asia, turns back, dreams only of Provençal literature and its gentle landscapes:

Sounge i felibre esteba. . . . I think of the starry *Félibres. . . .*[74]

It is the distinguishing trait of good artisans of Diversity to make a complete turnaround. Will Diversity ever be reached? This would be ruin, death. Diversity is always born anew in this artisan: he goes suddenly backward when in front there are arms stretched outward toward him.

Once there, however, Boissière writes about *Buddha, the Cemetery of Annam,* etc.[75]

In 1896, one year before his death, he wrote wonderful lines about exoticism in reverse:

Today, tired of awaiting the kiss of the Sirens, —My weary Flesh re-

turns to the village of my birth — Where the World's Echo captivates me still. . . .[76]

There, wandering, smoke from chimneys writhes: it is former desires and ancient sins burning.[77]

TIEN-TSIN, 1911.

Exoticism is really not the domain of exotic novelists but of great artists. True exoticism is not to be found in the language of Nolly,[78] of the Leblonds. But is so evidently present in the language of Anatole France,[79] of Maurice de Guérin, somewhat in Boissière's. Exotic criticism doesn't have to do with ocean liners, with Farrère and others.[80] But with Kipling, Le Roy...

"In my estimation, there is to date only a single man among the moderns who has found a language with which to speak of antiquity: he is Maurice de Guérin." (Goncourt.)[81]

I am the only one of my kind. The prose of *Les Xipéhuz,* which can be contrasted to that of *Les Immémoriaux,* is tainted by turns of phrase like the following: "it was year one thousand of these children peoples." And what is this "large, *ante*cuneiform book"? In any event, any notion of exoticism is shamefully shattered by this passage: "One must read the wonderful translation of Dessault, etc." right in the text.[82]

The Rosnys are the first to tire of their own grating style. Style. The first few pages are packed with unnecessary neologisms: "massing."[83] The last pages are quite run-of-the-mill.

The language of the Rosnys: "Wily ellipses of varying colors," "the cylinders of the stratums *rustled* like water thrown upon a flame."[84]

In summary, *Les Xipéhuz* presents a subject or an idea, which, with greater care, greater density, and, especially a greater sense of exoticism, would have been greatly improved. What I conceive to be my own exotic form has greater quality, caliber, dignity, homogeneity, and harmony.

TIEN-TSIN, 2 JUNE 1911.

Geographic exoticism. The upset, the disenchanting quality of the spherical world as opposed to the flat world.

Cosmas Indikopleustês, a Greek monk who was a sailor in his youth, was able to write (summing up knowledge in the sixth century): "The country that produces silk (China) is the farthest country, beyond India, well beyond Taprobane island. It is called Tzinitza. The ocean borders it on the East as well. The sages of India say that a line drawn from that country to the Empire would traverse Persia, and divide the world in two. The path to Tzinitza, which is much shorter by land than by sea, passes through Persia. Beyond the land of Tzinitza there is no possibility of sailing nor land inhabited by men. . . . Taprobane is the world's central market. Ships coming from India, Persia, Ethiopia, and Tzinitza bring their merchandise there: silk, eagle wood, cloves, sandalwood, pepper, etc."

Historical Works, translated by Wieger.

On a spherical surface, to leave one point is already to begin *to draw closer to it!* The sphere is Monotony. The poles are but a fiction. Does the center alone remain? with its weightlessness.

This is where tourism began! From the moment man realized the world was a sphere. "Tourism" would be the general name for a bad exotic attitude. The same goes for part of the vocabulary of travel. Translate it into my true *exoticism.* Nostalgia, equipment above all, sailors' terminology.

Excerpt from a letter to Henry Manceron, written in Tientsin on 23 September 1911.[85]

My very dear Henry,

I knew you were headed for La Manche, but I did not believe conditions would be so favorable for departure;[86] the hidden new joy of your letter reassured me completely. Like you, I think this move a happy one and am delighted it took place at just the right moment. But then, is there not great and beautiful asceticism in every departure? And finally, very egotistically, the departure which takes you away from there brings you closer to us, so that from this very moment we imagine your arrival here. You promise to come, do you not? You will have your own room and be among the large, black, lacquered chests decorated with golden dragons, and with porcelain reds, blues, and greens covering the bluish paste of old Ming. We await your arrival. Thanks to you, the coming year takes on a definite shape.

Even better, we will no doubt take you to Peking as soon as you arrive. I remain violently nostalgic for Peking. Trust me: scorn the coast. Forget Shanghai and the ports along the lower river. The edge of China has "advanced" like the bruised surface of a fruit. Inside, the pulp is still delicious.

Let us return to the tropics. And first of all, I must say that I always marvel at how, with often different conclusions and different sympathies than my own, your way of thinking is infinitely closer to my own than the thinking of those who might simply like what I like. The aim of a novel or a painting has as little importance as the aim of a discussion. But the quality *of those who discuss! — You paint your several hours in the "tropics" — though you were not drawn to return to them — with strong and exquisite strokes that move me, I who am still under their spell. Let us first separate "tropics" from "exoticism." The further I go, the more I realize how indispensable it is to my friends and to me that I write my* Essay on Exoticism. *I told you I had been happy in the tropics. This is violently true. During the two years I spent in Polynesia, I could hardly sleep for joy.*[87] *I would awake and cry in drunken joy at the break of day. Only the gods-of-pleasure know to what extent the moment of waking heralds the coming of day and reveals the continual happiness which the day lavishes. I felt exhilaration flowing through my muscles. I thought with pleasure; I discovered Nietzsche; I had my work under control, I was free, convalescent, fresh, and sensually quite experienced. I had some brief departures, some painful moments, some momentous and moving reunions. The whole island came to me like a woman. And, in fact, I had from women there such offerings as one no longer receives in any country nowadays. Besides the classic Maori wife, whose skin is soft and fresh, whose hair is sleek, whose mouth is muscular, I experienced caresses, meetings with lovers, and freedoms which asked nothing of me but voice, eyes, mouth, and pleasing childlike phrases. It is high time that I reassert my belief before maturity: the young girl, the virgin, is the only true lover in my eyes; she is so unknowing, or so cleverly and exquisitely hypocritical! I can still say this at the age of thirty-three, especially after twenty years of uninterrupted tastings; if I am still saying this in twenty years, my friends, at least, will know that this is not the onset of senility speaking, but the expression of my frankest amorous attitude.* My Essay on Exoticism *will reiterate this sentiment: the young girl is as far as can be from us, and therefore incomparably precious for all the devotees of diversity.*[88]

The nocturnal experiences I had in Tahiti were—without describing specific gestures—radiantly beautiful; —various perfumes intermingled with these moments, certainly; but I know exactly why I was so happy there. I also know that in five or ten years, when I return to live there and to write my story Maître-du-Jouir, *I will rediscover, though in different guises— (Oh! there will be no private passions)—analogous moments. Otherwise, I would not be worthy of feeling and living on.*

Here, it is true, the "senses" are not in a state of happiness. Whereas Peking atoned by its imperiality for the gloomy sadness of its dirty orgies and their husky female singers, Tientsin is provincial, Swiss or Belgian. In my stubbornness, I am constructing within myself, brick by brick, an interior Kiosk where existence would be less abject. But the very effort of constructing it prevents me at times from taking pleasure in inhabiting it.

I am slowly continuing to write Le Fils du Ciel.[89] *As to the preface to* Stèles, *it is done.*[90] *It seems rigorous in appearance, but is simply the description of the classical Chinese stele: its history, its uses, its devolutions; I have attempted to write it so that each word has a double meaning and resonates profoundly. I had thought of presenting these writings as translations as you suggest. Pierre Louÿs and Mérimée; yes.*[91] *—But what use is it to start over again? Anyhow, I prefer ambiguity. The reader will delve into that ambiguity himself.*

As my first stele prose poems have not displeased you, I enclose another, which is representative enough; it opens the fifth and last part of my book, which will be entitled (the part, that is) The Empire of the Middle.[92] *Here also is my official seal, nien hao, or if you prefer, its slogan, which will also be the justification for the printing run of the book:*

年心経
成宣朔

which reads: Wou tch'ao Sin Siuan-nien-tch'eng and translates as: Completed during the Sin Siuan period (or of the promulgation of the empire of the heart) of the dynasty "without dynastic succession."[93]

These words encapsulate the main idea of "Sans marque de Règne," of "Perdre le midi," and of the entire book, in which the transfer of the Empire of China onto the Empire of the Self is continuous.

18 OCTOBER 1911, TIENTSIN.

On Exoticism and an Aesthetics of Diversity.
On Exoticism as an Aesthetics of Diversity.
Essay on Exoticism: An Aesthetics of Diversity.

I will not conceal it: this book will disappoint most readers. Despite its exotic title, it cannot be about such things as the tropics or coconut trees, the colonies or Negro souls, nor about camels, ships, great waves, scents, spices, or enchanted islands. It cannot be about misunderstandings and native uprisings, nothingness and death, colored tears, oriental thought, and various oddities, nor about any of the preposterous things that the world "Exoticism" commonly calls to mind. Even less so can it be about those writers who gave Exoticism this meaning. For it is in this way that "Exoticism" became compromised and bloated. In fact, it is now so bloated that it is about to explode, to burst, to empty itself of its contents. It would have been wiser to avoid such a dangerous term — a term so charged and yet so ambiguous — and to forge another one in order to reroute or break with these lesser meanings. But I preferred to take the risk and keep this term, which still seemed good and solid to me despite the bad uses to which it had been put. After giving it a thorough delousing, I wanted to try to restore to it — along with its initial value — all the primacy it once possessed. Thus rejuvenated, I dare believe it will possess that unpredictable quality of a neologism without partaking of a neologism's sourness or acidity. Exoticism. It should be understood that I mean only one thing, but something immense by this term: the feeling which Diversity stirs in us.

Moreover, may it be understood that this work is not an assertion so much as a search. If I undertake to write it, it is not in order to display fully formed ideas but in order to help me think this matter through in the way I intend to; that is, to bring the entire human triad into play, to feel intensely and act accordingly. Then, all this discussion will lead me to the final, agonizing question in the last chapter: the question of Exoticism's decline in the world. I am writing this book in order to reassure myself. I am writing in order to convince myself — in order to say "yes" forcefully to myself from the very outset — even though I do not know whether this affirmation will be conclusive (whether this "yes" will be utterable later). Had I believed that the quantity of Exoticism in the world were stable or on the rise, I would have been content to take pleasure in it, and — what for writers amounts to the same thing — simply to express it bluntly in order to communicate this pleasure to others. But, from the depths of my sincerity today, the day when this preface is completed, I cannot say if Exoticism is on the rise or on the wane. It is in order to be able to determine its true state in the world with certainty that I present and attempt to link my thoughts in this particular way. I will then be free to allow my desire to orient the answer. I will even be free to deny it, if it is a disheartening one.

One should not attempt to arrive at this conclusion directly, in one fell swoop, thereby omitting the steps which lead to it. This could take away all value from the answer because the question would also be deprived of value. Exoticism is not something which simply grabs you by the throat; you have to arouse it slowly, so as, later, to allow yourself to be embraced by it.

[In the margin] This is nothing but an unresolved question at this point; it will be clarified not by the reading of this book but by the very process of its composition. I know where I want to go: but this very destination is itself a bifurcation, an uncertainty. And perhaps this uncertainty is a negative one if it is painful.

[In the margin] This partakes of the journal form. All the steps are there, it is true; but we are going to extend the path together. The lesson to be learned is not known in advance.

[In the margin] There is a dreadful expression, I no longer know where it comes from: "*The Entropy of the Universe tends toward a maximum.*"[94] This notion has weighed upon me — in my youth, my adolescence, my awakening. Entropy: it is the sum of all internal, nondifferentiated forces, all static forces, all the lowly forces of energy. I do not know if the latest advances in thought on this subject refute or confirm it. But I imagine Entropy as a yet more terrifying monster than Nothingness. Nothingness is made of ice, of the cold. Entropy is lukewarm. Nothingness is diamond-like, perhaps. Entropy is pasty. A lukewarm paste.

21 OCTOBER 1911. TIENTSIN.

Gloss. Bernardin de Saint-Pierre![95] I have read him only here, in Tientsin, seven years later. No doubt quoted [an illegible word here] contempt for his insipidity. Loti? Already anticipated.

"Include the fewest number of quotations possible" — Not one. Oh! not one. Already well noted: Parallelism between stepping back in time (Historicism) and moving out in space (Exoticism). André Gide says: *The Epoch* is equivalent to the notion of Homeland. "Yes, sir, an important epoch . . . and how could I not find my own epoch admirable. . . . Yes, I ask that I be allowed to admire my epoch in the way that Barrès loves his native Lorraine. . . ."[96] Please understand only that the *epoch,* just like the *homeland.* . . ."[97]

In summary, not too much nostalgia or desire for something else, but, rather, a lively and immediate pleasure of living in a particular epoch in relation to others. Always reinforce individualism.

While experiencing China profoundly, I have never had the desire to be Chinese. While I have felt the force of the Vedic dawn, I have never really regretted not being born three thousand years earlier and a herdsman. Take off from the real, from what is, from what one is. Homeland. Epoch.

Gloss. Take up from that first entry the study of the senses from an exotic point of view and discuss also the exoticism of the senses among themselves. (Exoticism between the different arts.)

Already noted: *Sexual exoticism.*

Sidestep the danger later: the collaboration with Pierre Richard who himself, in any event, neglected it.[98]

21 OCTOBER 1911. TIENTSIN.

(Last Chapter)
Of Essential Exoticism

If, by any chance, some have followed me to this point, they should leave me on the path at this very juncture. By the very promise I made to them, I must see it through to the end; but this promise does not oblige them as it does me. A sudden breathlessness, an irresponsible cramp, a lack of muscular preparedness may occur. And we are entering regions where it is difficult to breathe, rarefied and icy regions.

To this point, there were good provisions: sensations which became warmer and sharper. These end here, and we will only experience their pale and insubstantial reflection. Nevertheless, it is a wager. I promised to go.

Here, then, the subject receives almost all its fullness from the object which it envelops. But the object, certainly, has not yet disappeared. We know well that it will never disappear. Yet we have here a spectacle of Difference where it is still difficult to perceive it: everything appears to take place in the mind. This is the spectacle of Antinomies.

Verbally, if one believes in the words, how exoticism is intensified by antinomies. Ideas which are not simply different, but diametrically opposed to each other! If flavor increases as a function of difference, what could be more flavorful than the opposition between irreducible entities, the shock of eternal contrasts?

And yet, if one contemplates it, what harshness, what dryness: White and black. Black and white. (Analysis: the ability to feel Diversity entails, I must have already said, two phases of which one is reducible: one of the divergent elements is ourselves. In the other phase, we observe a difference between two parts of the object. This second phase must lead back to the first if one desires to turn it into the sensation of exoticism: then, the subject weds and merges with one of the component parts of the object for a time, and Diversity bursts forth between this and the other part of the object. Otherwise there is no exoticism. A subject's realization of the dual nature of the Object does not bring forth the birth of diversity. It consists simply of an intellectual operation of a mathematical order of the simplest kind: addition; or in library science: the catalogue. This is the beginning of the most honorable exact sciences. It is not Exoticism.)

In the presence of these Antinomies, of categorical oppositions, the Mind will have to decide on a course of action. Will it be able to? Well or poorly? In a continuous or discontinuous way? and many other questions…. An affinity is difficult. The drawing of lots is not very convincing. The observer will be drawn neither to one nor to the other. Exoticism will not spring forth.

An attitude of contemplation will probably replace it. This attitude utters words of death. The joy that one claims is complete joy, is as hard to attain as the pain of displeasure. A child cried out in terror at the solemn, eternal, frozen description of complete and heavenly joy. Hell frightened him less.

(Or: having arrived at these high and icy summits, the conscious subject will be content to turn his gaze from one summit to the other without truly enjoying the goodness and beauty of his physical efforts.) (Footnote: The power and novelty of muscular imagery in Claudel. The rebirth of muscular sensation.)

(End this chapter by somewhat ironically opposing the essential law of Bovarysm, which will perhaps be the only quotation in the book, to these philosophical considerations, which are lacking in Exotic content. Perhaps cite only the words of Jules de Gaultier: "And he delighted in diversity" [recaptured].)

[WITHOUT A DATE, PROBABLY 1912]

Beside the state of Knowing, institute the state of *perceptiveness,* not nihilist, not destructive.

12 APRIL 1912.

Expertise and the collection.

Bringing together objects whose only quality, sometimes, is that they differ slightly from each other is still to pay homage —if somewhat crudely—to Difference. The collector vulgarly thinks, or is believed to, that he is gathering together a group of objects which are "similar" or analogous to each other.... What a mistake! All the interest resides in Difference. The finer the Difference, the more difficult it is to discern, the greater the awakening and stimulation of the feeling for Diversity. Red and green? Not at all! Red and reddish, then red and another red with an infinite number of gradations. The conglomeration of objects facilitates a "discerning" judgment, facilitates "discernment." Every series, every gradation, every comparison engenders variety, diversity. Separated from each other, objects seemed vaguely similar, homogenous; placed side by side, they are opposed to each other, or, at least, they "exist" with all the more force because matter, richer and more supple, has more means and nuanced modalities.

4 JANUARY 1913.

Without cultivating the paradox, I must accept it or even pose it when it is necessary to do so. The positive portion of this book, its foundation, its springboard, must first be a pure negation: I must remove from the word "Diversity," and especially from the word "Exotic," all the too-positive notions with which they were laden up to now. I must vacate the premises and then dust them off in order to attempt not the filling up of the wineskin, which has remained empty and smelling a little of vinegary wine, but the puncturing of the wineskin itself, so that no one will speak of it again. Thus the word exoticism will have recovered its original purity and will signify nothing but the feeling of experiencing the purity and intensity of Diversity.

5 JANUARY 1913.

Brush aside all literary criticism.

Even in my analysis of the most colorful tropical exoticism, I will rule out, of my own accord, the use of quotations from authors, whether in order to praise them or vilify them. Unless it is used systematically or cynically, a quotation is only extraneous in a book relating the progression of ideas, where I take it as a lack or absence of tact; a word (borrowed, not cited, from a trade association) always gives the feel of it being "plated." This plated word can work if used systematically, whereby it becomes an "inlaid work." Later on, and, elsewhere, above all, I will systematize this somewhat basic structure of my work and engage in literary criticism. But at this point, it would displease me to invite to my cabinetmaking either mediocre workers or great artists, whom I prefer not to smash to pieces. It is rare, in any event, that a quotation carries a weight commensurate with all its power. More often, it crushes the text which surrounds it, and the reader has only one desire as a result: to prolong its impact by turning right to the author being cited. Another and more delicate matter is that of "allusion." Literary allusion is a rather delicate play of ideas, a citation in veiled form... (but not too often: *cliché, proverb,* at least for Chinese literary Allusions, reexamined in this connection). I will often have recourse to allusion. At the very least, it does not break up the sentence's own sonority.

Exoticism is really a principle of the same order as Bovarysm, but is perhaps secondary to Bovarysm, if one understands it to mean a *"Creative Error."* Eternal Bovarysm or power (I would say an initial metaphysical undertaking) having created existence by means of Diversity, having produced Diversity, we must now undertake to valorize Diversity in its various forms. From this nearness of nature, a connection perhaps, but I do not know yet, a nearness, a community of effects. Everything that Jules de Gaultier says about Bovarysm or about the Creative Error can be applied word for word to diversity. This is not a quotation but a sort of word for word transliteration: "The role of *Diversity* as a creative principle for all psychological reality has been perceived by all the *great* writers, playwrights, etc., as a more or less distinct vision. The total history of literature should be written from this perspective of *Diversity.* This history would thereby be granted a sense of order, a clarity, a generality, that no other system of classification has been able to grant it up to this time, because such a concept has nothing about it that is fortuitous, accidental, or borrowed from external considerations. Rather, it dominates any ordering of facts and of circumstances by its psychological character, because it is interior to the object discussed in whatever expression of literary effort."[99]

Begin with the work of Lafcadio Hearn, well-read tourist of Japan. Excuse myself from tackling someone who is dead. Specify that these essays of literary criticism do not demand a perfect knowledge of the object, in this case, Japan; I will only strive to judge a literary attitude here, no more.

1913.

The decline of Diversity.

It seems that *yes*. Like Energy, the Entropy of the Universe tends towards a maximum.

But slowly. Is this a human grandeur? We may lament it. If I witness this process, I may experience distress. If it is of the same order as a civilized evolution, as a discovery. I am thirty-five years old, only at the half point of my life, and already I have experienced the unknown and discovered Pole; I will witness the division of Panama and Tahiti starting from the center....

Or if we are speaking about a cosmological order of phenomena: the progress toward Hercules; the abating of solar fever... this is no longer very human, and really it would be very artificial to feel compassion for such things.

Well, sadly, I think that the decline of exoticism is on a scale of great human events.... But also that the ability to taste even the weakest flavor of diversity is increasing, which, perhaps, compensates for this decline?

Excerpt from a letter to Henry Manceron,
written in Tchang-te-fou on 3 February 1913

And, first of all, I cannot but prove you right when you see in Stèles *a spontaneous refutation of the attitude of* literary *exoticism that I have explained to you before; not a refutation: the rupturing of the formula. I only attempted to express myself there. I must say that exoticism made the task a lot easier for me: in allowing me not to speak about certain "topics" — I mistrust this — but in giving me a form, settings, a new decor. Another step and the "Stele" would entirely lose for me its Chinese origin in order to represent plainly and accurately: a new literary genre — like the novel, previously, which came forth or not from a certain* Princesse de Clèves, *or from further back still, and arriving at* Salammbô, *then at everything, then at nothing at all.*[100] *It is possible that later on, a long time from now, I will write another collection of Steles, and that they will contain nothing at all of China, not even the paper. Like the genre of the "elegy," which does not prejudge the nationality of the tears that are shed. Like the Pindaric ode singing if need be of a Christian god. You know from long ago my striving not to repeat myself: from* Les Immémoriaux, *objective or claiming to be, I have jumped to* Maître du Jouir *whose first word is the word "I." But I think the steps are more pronounced here. I indicate two additional ones. The second,* Peintures, *will be more conclusive perhaps, more insistent, more unexpected.*[101] Stèles *can perhaps be called a collection of prose poems, even if the rectangle which contains them outlines rather severely what used to be an elastic genre.*[102] Peintures *will not have a defined name already in the Nisards, Lansons, Deschamps, and Nordaûs.*[103] *If I had to give it a name, I could find nothing other than "Patters," or perhaps "Parade of Easels."*[104] *This is in any case the very title of the preface. A gathering of spectators who must be enticed, and of large canvases with bright, sometimes garish colors (but one will not know if it is red paint or blood) that one must comment upon, "make others see." Here, because I am dealing with literature, there are no canvases, and the words all alone must not only conjure up an image but* create the image. *From which arises the need for the ascendancy of a speaker, of an Exhibitor for the wide-eyed spectators.... A magical half-power. Raw evocations. Verbal phantasmagorias; and, suddenly, retraction and the gray wall. The subjects? The whole of Chinese history. The form: the varied one of Chinese painting, hangings or horizontal scrolls; the material: sometimes lacquer, porcelain.... But everything must submit to the fundamental attitude: a Patter.*

The Odes: Capitol or a rock that is well known. My one effort will be to keep geese from entering.

Yes, "indifferent to China," as the precious and spontaneous judgment of Riquette says;[105] *I try to be: Limiting oneself to China and clinging only to China would be a sign of decay, and a cowardly limitation, even if China is powerful and inexhaustible. —And it is not the least of the merits of this large, immensely "exotic" continent, to have made my very own exoticism burst forth.*

As a literary *attitude, I mean. Because it has remained intact as a play of ideas which is strictly philosophical in nature. I will surely write that "Essay on Exoticism" "as an Aesthetics of Diversity," the first outlines of which I have already burdened you with in Cherbourg, I think. —But*

*what good is it even telling you of the ditch that I am digging between a
philosophical mechanism and the free play of words and of senses.*

6 MAY 1913. TIENTSIN.

Manuscript resulting from a marching order to produce one
page per day on average.

Of Exoticism as an Aesthetics of Diversity

I know and do not hide it: this book will disappoint most
readers. Despite its already somewhat compromised title, it will
not have much about the tropics or palm trees, coconut trees,
Asian palm trees, or guava trees, unknown fruits and flowers;
nor about monkeys with human faces and Negros who act like
monkeys; the reader will not experience any "great swells" or
scents, or spices; unless it is as spices themselves, or, quite precisely, as appetizers, crudely preparing one for something more
substantial. I will navigate few cruises through those islands
furthest removed from the world. A few colored tears will be
shed there, but their quantity will soon dry up. I will not de-
plore "incomprehensibilities," but, on the contrary, praise them
to the utmost. Most importantly, the book will not be about
budgets and administrations; though the worst curse that could
fall upon this book would be for it to be forever dismembered,
confused with, perhaps even celebrated in good faith under the
rubric "colonial," and classified as colonial literature.

For all this is actually part of what is understood today to
be contained within the word which is the work's point of departure: Exoticism. A bloated and compromised word, abused,
ready to explode, to burst, to empty itself of everything. I would
have done well to avoid such a dangerous word, such an ambiguous word. Should I forge another? Would it have had the
fortune and inevitability of "Bovarysm," whose master, to
whom this refers and is joined, is he who allows me to think,

who has imposed both idea and form? I preferred to take up the challenge and to keep what still seemed fundamentally good about this word despite its sullying; but in doing so I tried first to delouse it, and in the harshest fashion, so as to return to it, along with its former value, all the primacy of its initial flavor. Thus rejuvenated, I dare believe it will have the enticing green quality of a neologism without taking on a neologism's bitterness or acidity. *Exoticism:* may it be said that by this word I mean only a single yet universal thing: the feeling which Diversity stirs in me; and, aesthetically, the practice of this very feeling; its pursuit, its play, its greatest freedom; its greatest intensity; finally, its most brilliant and profound beauty.

"One might be tempted" to entrust a portion of this research to the analysis and searches already completed about the nature and the essence of things, and, especially, about the composition of matter. I am tempted to do this. I am coming to this. I ask therefore the extensive support of all that exists, whether this heart of everything is the homogenous or the diverse. It seems that one answer is certain. If the homogenous prevails in the deepest reality, nothing prevents one from believing in its eventual triumph over sensory reality, that which we touch, finger, clutch, and devour with all our teeth and with all the buds of our senses. Then the way will be cleared for the Kingdom of the Lukewarm; that moment of viscous mush without inequalities, falls, or reboundings, was prefigured grotesquely by the disappearance of ethnographic diversity. If, happily, diversity begins to manifest itself more and more acutely as a result of our insistence and understanding of it, then there is hope. We should have faith that some *fundamental* differences will never end up being a real fabric without some sewing or restitching of fragments; and that the increasing fusion, the destruction of barriers, the great short cuts through space, must of their own accord compensate themselves by means of new partitions and unforeseen lacuna, a system of very fine filigree striated through the fields that one initially perceived as an unbroken space. Yes, let us explore matter. All the same, with the confidence and skepticism mixed together in equal quantities of he who throws a coin and bets on heads, sees it fall on tails, and begins again. If matter answers no, we will nevertheless force it to answer "yes."

And here it turns out that, of its own accord, matter itself answers "yes." It is an obliging friend, for a time. I am not concealing what I call "matter." Is it the eternal "substance" or not? Is it divisible or not? Complete or filled with gaps?... or whatever we want it to be? I call "matter" the idea that I have gleaned from research done in the time period in which I live and to which I am bound. I call "matter" that which the works of Thomson, Einstein, Svante Arrhemius, W. Ostwald, Jean Perrin, Pierre Weiss, and the Curies have yielded to me at little cost. This matter, guaranteed by its newness, patented by the different governments which appointed these observers, is sufficient for me and delights me with the answer it gives me: it instructs me about the discontinuous nature of the world. It teaches me that the world's structure is "infinitely" granular and negates the rigorous application of mathematical continuity to reality.

Excerpt from a letter to Jules de Gaultier,
written in Peking on 11 January 1914.

My journey is decidedly taking on for me the quality of a sincere experience—a confrontation, in the field, between the imaginary and the real: the mountain as seen by the "Poet," and the same mountain climbed by someone to whom it forbids passage, and, who will find on the other side of the pass, after ten hours of ascent, something to eat, a place to sleep, and, perhaps (but will he concern himself with this?), the added comfort of a beautiful vision.... And the running waters of the river, traversed, not as on a map, but from its source to its mouth....

Then I will have acquired, I hope, the right to come to a decision: at least to lean toward the fictive side—memories and schemes—when my bones and my muscles will already have given what they must. At the expense of ten months of effort and travel, I will look for the personal right to a rest or withdrawal, to a long, concentric meditation without a goal. Even what is pretentious about these words is excusable if one considers the concrete work which will follow.

This concreteness is promising: a very beautiful journey. For four months, the unknown in time: the past, to be apprehended; then five months: the space to be delineated in small drawings. You already know Voisins. Our third companion is just as much one of us: Jean Lartigue, your devotee;[106] *a contemplative mind with an utterly frank and youthful body. Few people will have been as well suited to each other at the point of departure; better: openly affectionate, and by experience.*

3 JUNE 1916.

The Human — The Superhuman — The Inhuman

The man who takes himself as the measure of all things is soon disappointed. He names this disappointment the virtue of humility. (He makes a virtue of his disappointment.) The man who sees himself as the measure of all things is, whether he wants it or not, an artist. He creates works as man creates men. To turn toward god, to make one's god, is not really leaving the human. It is choosing among human qualities a group of sometimes disparate qualities, like Goodness and Justice, and making of these qualities a monster with divergent feelings, like one of those Shivas with twelve arms. But I have spoken elsewhere of the exoticism of the divine. It is through a path diverging from that one, differing in its desire for the divine, that I intend to make a path leading to the deified Diversity, the miraculous and capable Diversity, the inspiring Diversity: The Inhuman.

A step, or rather an exalted moment, which gives the genesis of this feeling all the expansion of a birth , and more organs and more and stronger muscles: this step is the Superhuman. Let us accept the definition of the originator of the word. His definitions. That man tends toward the Superhuman....[107] Granted.

All this is nothing but an expansion, not an escape; an increase, but not going as far as producing the unforgettable shock of Diversity. Like the word within the word, the superhuman is still human.

In order to get to the Inhuman, it is not enough to be human. I want, first, to cleanse that word: inhumanity, that is, cruelty, crudeness, the contrary of humanity understood as goodness; these qualities are always the more humane virtues of the human animal.... Let us not imitate the Chinese ("of the limpid and fine heart") who gave to one of their richest types, in Kiang-Ye, "that most male of types, more manly than all men — the posthumous nickname of the Inhuman." [108]

(In this way, I will proceed by citing only selected quotations in my text. Less because of pride than because it is natural for me to do so and in order to avoid a marquetry or inlaid effect in my text: which is not that of the Mosaic (The Mosaic? so be it; but not marquetry). Reject everything else, unless it is brief and can be reduced to a word or two.)

(The inhuman. What is other than a man. One can be made aware of it less by the direct feeling which it inspires, than by a search for this feeling. Do not confuse it with the Absolute.

The Inhuman: its real Name is the Other. It thus becomes not a god but an action that is inherent in thought.... To imagine as a function of the adverse.)

Sacrifice: considered as the positive Tasting of Diversity. In Debauchery, suddenly deny the flesh: tasting Debauchery. In chaste tranquillity, exalt in Erotic joys. Monastic practice: they were connoisseurs.

In this instance, sacrifice is *beautiful,* that is, in relation to Diversity.

21 APRIL 1917, SHANGHAI.

Imago Mundi

Here are the First Things, beneath which there is Nothing.

Of Exoticism. Its personal justification. Its universal power: if I place Exoticism at the center of my vision of the world, if I take pleasure in seeking it, exalting it, creating it when I cannot find it; signaling its existence to those who are worthy of it and who are on the lookout for it—those who are worthy of it and who did not have an idea of it—it is not because Exoticism is a unique aesthetic force, but because it is a fundamental Law of the Intensity of *Sensation,* of the exaltation of Feeling; and therefore of living.

It is through Difference and in Diversity that existence is made glorious.

a) My personal search for Exoticism: First, my travels, the most childish; but which yielded that pure work: *Les Immémoriaux. Upon my return,* and before *departing once again,* the extension of geographic Exoticism to a *System* encompassing the world.

When I conceived of this book, I thought it was simply a "way of seeing," my own; and I took on the task of simply conveying the way the world seemed to me in its most flavorable aspect: in it diversities. Quinton had said to me: "I think each one of us is capable of saying only one thing." And I was aware of sinking into the innumerable in order to grasp the One—and to express it. I thought, too, that this would lead me to create works which would be full of flavor for some. This was a second period. China: *Stèles, Peintures.*

b) But certain ideas that are the result of certain general observations (Turkish revolution, Chinese revolution, Russian revolution, indeed, even the Great War) lead me to grant my theory of Exoticism greater general validity. I do not wish it to be inferior in *Catholicism* to Claudel's *giant* idea; in its taking part of the Sea; of the Waters; of the Mind. And I now realize, in this state of Solitude, that it is much more vast than I first

thought; and that it encompasses—*whether they wish it or not*—
ALL MEN, MY BROTHERS—WHETHER I WISH IT OR NOT.

For in searching instinctively for Exoticism, I have sought
Intensity, Power, that is, Life. (I think it is useless to demean
myself by explaining once more what others, precursors, have
attained: the Value of Life. Some have said it; others have lived
it.)

It is in seeing how diverse values tend to intermingle, to come
together, to become defiled, that I understood how all men
were submissive to the Law of Exoticism. It is because of the
Debasement of Exoticism on the surface of the Earth that I re-
solved to convene all men, my brothers—so that they will feel
it a little, this law, which I first thought to be only a personal
aesthetics.

After the Great War, my influence on them could be to show
them that if they have fought previously against each other it
was for weak values, values destined to become weaker still:
their diversities become a kind of lowly antagonism.

The exotic Tension of the World is decreasing. Exoticism, a
source of Energy—mental, aesthetic, or physical (though I do
not like to mix levels)—is on the wane.

—It so happens that at the very moment I have arrived at the
clear conviction that my personal aesthetics is a doctrine good
for all, efficacious, active (leaving aside, logically, the entire
metaphysics of Brahma, all *confusion* in a loved or divine object),
it turns out that I realize, at the same time, that its Progress, its
Rate, is in a state of decline in the world! —(Cf. the old formula
noted beforehand: The Entropy of the Universe tends toward
a maximum.)

—The means of Wearing Down Exoticism on the surface
of the Globe: everything we call Progress. The laws of applied
physics; mechanical modes of travel making people confront
each other, and—horror—intermingling them, mixing them
up without making them fight each other. The undeniable weakening of Religions. Where are the martyrs? Or perhaps they are

replaced (but Péguy was a soldier) by those who died for a reason whose roots are known....[109] —Where is the mystery? — Where are the distances?

There used to be a considerable distance between the Tsar and the muzhik—the Son of Heaven and the people, despite the paternal theory: ancient courts, the small courts of Germany, or the princely cities of Italy were some of Diversity's beautiful tools.[110] The rule of the people brings with it the same customs, the same functions everywhere.

—But one cannot let oneself go in this way: to react at the very moment when Exoticism declines. Lilith was right: "Lord, give me man!"—*unnamable Lord of the world, give me the Other!— The div... no, the Diverse. For the Divine is but another one of man's games.*

So Diversity is in decline. Men are in conflict among themselves, that is to say, battling known and steady forces, wherein it is enough for one force to have greater weight than the other —$\frac{1}{2}mv^2$. Where is the mysterious within, the mysterious, which is the quivering approach, the extraordinary scent of Diversity before it triumphs as such! —There is nothing mysterious in this war.

Diversity is in decline. Therein lies the great earthly threat.

It is therefore against this decay that we must fight, fight amongst ourselves—perhaps die with beauty.

Poets and visionaries are always engaged in this battle, be it in the depths of their own selves, or—and I am suggesting this— against the walls of Knowledge: Space and Time, Law and Causality. Against the limits of Knowledge. There, for man, the smallest gap would be so much more important than the break through the Hindenburg line! —This is what must not be said; —hardly written.[111]

—Cure for the Decline of the rate of exoticism: praise the partial exotic values which remain. Woman (absolute condemnation of feminism, a kind of monstrous social inversion). Praise the fantastic, profound, and unknown past. (Research into the Time of past Ages.) View the future only with caution and irony. Is the future exotic??? Futurist novels give me the sensation of model mannequins being taken for statues.

—Well, World-Almighty, which way should we turn?

—Write at last a series of essays in this Note. Henceforth, compare everything to this Note.

—But, perhaps, in some other parts of the Universe, new Diverse worlds are coming into existence. (See notecard: cold contraction Adiabat.)

—The first voyage around the world must have been the most disenchanting. Luckily, Magellan died before his return. As for his pilot, he simply completed his task without worrying about that horrific thing: there was no longer an utter Remoteness in the world!

—What is gained here: Diversity, a source of general energy. Cold pole and hot pole. Potential. Exchanges. Work.

8 OCTOBER 1917, DEPARTING FROM HAÏPHONG.

Book One: The Decline of Diversity.
Book Two: Diversity as the source of all energy.
Book Three: The Re-integration of Diversity.

Thus this entire work will become a drama. A book in action: Report—Despair—Revival.

The Decline of Exoticism. Send out such Jeremiads with desperate prophecies. Take geographic diversity as an initial, crude example, the only one people are familiar with, the only one which has preoccupied people. Show that it is the only one in a state of decline. Then go through various exoticisms on the wane. Geographic. Then those *within* man: the exoticism of God for man, of heroes for man, of the King for his people. All this is in full decline. Exoticism of war in decline. (Logical thinking about war, but only in relation to exoticism, because this exoticism is a total effort, the facet of a mirror I cast over all the facts which surround me. War is a fact.)

Exoticisms that are intact or potential exoticisms: Woman, Music, and, in general, all artistic sentiment.

Who is the consoling god most different from humans? The inhuman.

Finish with the famous phrase: there is no servant who thinks of his master as a great man. But who is even speaking of servants: the concierge below. What gentleman friend would go asking the domestics for their opinion of "Monsieur"? The great man must not be debased but celebrated.

DECLINE — DECREASE

The Philosopher and his doctrine. If I speak, if I write, it is in order to be read and understood. There is no action that is as detached as this one. This paragraph is not just prose. Certainly, I would have to define what I mean by a philosopher secreting his philosophy; the philosopher who feeds himself on his philosophy. I do not wish my study to remain lifeless. Be it in a gesture, be it in a sound, I would be happy for it to be influential. — And even if certain chapters on woman could ever have been read by lovers in love, I would consider all praise to have been in vain.

THE FADING OF DIVERSITY

I do not pretend that what follows will be cheerful or comforting — nor apparently very new. Others have lamented approaching disasters; but they have neither said enough nor seen everything. The words used had already been used up. There were a whole range of symbols that were compromised. In the end, those lamenting only shed their tears around a single vessel, without recognizing that other, vaster urns called for similar distress.

We are speaking here of exoticism and its decline. I cannot in three words, after three lines, hope to define a word that has already been well used, well gauged, well compromised. But

I hope to get there in the course of writing these lines. Provisionally, Exoticism will be understood as the *manifestation of Diversity.*

(Failing to define Exoticism right away, and to say what it is according to my understanding, and my plan to understand it, I will hasten to say all that it is not. Before arriving at the sanctuary, one must clean the vestibule. If this measure seems fastidious, I nevertheless believe it to be indispensable.)

I

One of the simplest, crudest manifestations of Diversity, as it appears to man, is its geographical manifestation in climates, fauna, and flora. This is actually the only kind known to man by that name. It is a vulgarized Diversity, a Diversity within reach of everyone. It can serve as a magnifying example, and we must put an end to it, despite its vulgarity. As the only one that is known, it introduced false values: thanks to it, "colonial" and "exotic" have come to designate analogous values in a certain kind of literature; so that a David, encompassing the whole music of the immense desert within the procession of camels, or a White woman, making a Black man her lover, is thought to have done enough by changing color, or simply temperature....

The "colonial" is exotic, but exoticism surpasses the colonial by far.

(All these pleasantries about helmet, camel, bear music... reject them for later on.)

In brief, I will examine geographic exoticism here.

Two main trajectories, depending on whether one moves along the meridians or the parallels; depending on whether one moves from one of the poles toward the equator or along the parallels. I will call the first geographical Exoticism in latitude and the second geographical Exoticism in longitude. If one climbs or descends, it is an exoticism in altitude.

Finally, the mere enumeration of the three dimensions at least evokes the fourth, if not the number "n" of possible dimensions. But this, which does not really make up part of the globe, of the good, fat maternal globe—this is to be held in reserve... as another exoticism, no longer geographic but spatial. (Perhaps discuss the discovery of the roundness of planet Earth there.)

These various exoticisms have a hierarchy in the [illegible word here]. The most apparent and the first born is Exoticism in latitude. This exoticism can be held responsible for the camel, the Negro, the palm trees....

(Insert here a descriptive definition of the three Exoticisms (perhaps adding to them the exoticism of mountain to sea). Denser descriptions than those tranquil and logical hairsplitting arguments.) After making them *visible,* show their decline by the multiplicity of Travels.

A) Exoticism in latitude:

2 OCTOBER 1918, 10 P.M.

Exoticism as an Aesthetics of Diversity

I agree to call "Diverse" everything that until now was called foreign, strange, unexpected, surprising, mysterious, amorous, superhuman, heroic, and even divine, everything that is *Other;* —that is to say, in each of those words, emphasize the dominance of the *essential* Diversity that each of those terms harbors within it.

I continue to give to the word "aesthetics" its specific meaning, which is that of an exact science that the professional thinkers have imposed upon it and which it retains. It is at once the science of spectacle and the beautification of spectacle; it is the most marvelous tool of knowledge. It is knowledge which cannot be and should not be anything but a means, not of all the world's beauty, but of that aspect of beauty that each mind, whether it wants to or not, retains, develops, or neglects. This is the appropriate vision of the world. (An *Imago Mundi,* in this example: my own.)

In order to refer to the content of the book in its entirety and to enclose these two elements within a single title, the aesthetics of diversity, which constitutes but the subtitle, I have chosen a word that is in common usage, *Exoticism,* with the idea that its use, without prejudices of any kind, will take on all the new meanings with which this book must inflate it.

To this day, the word *Exoticism* has hardly been more than a synonym for "impressions of faraway lands"; of climates, of foreign races; and too often misused by being substituted for that word, which is yet more compromised, "colonial." Under the dreadful rubric of "exotic literature," "exotic impressions,"... one gathered, and one gathers still, all the flashy paraphernalia of a return from the abode of a Negro king; the crass, flashy rags of those who return from we know not where.... I cannot deny that there exists an exoticism of countries and races, an exoticism of climates, of fauna and flora; an exoticism that is subject to geography, to the position in latitude and longitude. It is this exoticism, specifically, which is most obvious and which imposed its name, giving to man, who was too inclined to consider himself as identical to himself at the beginning of his terrestrial adventure, the conception of other worlds than his own. The word is the result of this process. But the kind of insistence with which this kind of exoticism imposes itself upon those who travel, its too large visibility, makes it also a good point of departure and necessitates that I finish with it by dealing with it one last time. It will be the subject of the first chapter—necessary.

But the main body of the work is to go as fast as possible, as far as possible. The flow of thoughts will therefore not stop before reaching, by means of the steps that the titles of the following chapters have as their name, essential exoticism, the Law of effective Diversity. —Nothing would be said, nothing would be so....

End the "Foreword" with:

This, which is universal, is simply my own vision, an artist's: see the world, then put forth one's vision of the world.

Draft of the Plan[112]

The birth of Diversity.
The genesis of the External World.
The feeling of Diversity.
The flavor of Exoticism.

Exoticism of the Sexes.

Of the Expression of Diversity.
    By means of different senses....
    By means of different Arts. —It is for this reason that Exoti-
        cism is located within the different arts themselves. (Re-
        member the law I proclaim in the last chapter, that one
        cannot taste Diversity unless one weds oneself to a par-
        ticular perspective. Tasting the exoticism of different arts
        assumes that one takes a different side each time.)
    The author and his Expression of Diversity.
    Truly Exotic styles.
    (Cf. and take up again: the irksome author.)
    Possibility of a critical attitude, whose pivot point would be
        a pure, exotic attitude.

The Decline of Exoticism.
    Gobineau: *On Inequality.*[113]

Ethnogeographic Exoticism: from the day when one rediscovered that the Earth is round.

Tourism.

Exoticism of the Divine.

   a) in relation to mankind

   b) among Divine Beings themselves, on the condition that man commits himself to a single religion (see my law regarding the necessity of taking a position).

The exoticism of Nature.

Last chapter.

Universal Exoticism, or, better yet, essential Exoticism.

   Argument: the selected Notion, the feeling of Diversity, the special attitude of the subject for the object having embraced all thought, the thinking being (always according to the Hindu mechanism) finds himself face to face with himself. This is universal Exoticism, essential Exoticism. But here too, according to the essential Law of Bovarysm, he does not overlook the fact that, in conceiving of himself, he can conceive himself only as something *other* than he is.

                  And he rejoices in his diversity.

Notes

Foreword

1 Walter Benjamin, *Charles Baudelaire: A Lyric Poet in the Era of High Capitalism,* trans. Harry Zohn (London: Verso, 1983), p. 106.

2 Ibid.

3 Ibid., p. 105.

4 Ibid.

5 See Chris Bongie, *Exotic Memories: Literature, Colonialism, and the Fin de Siècle* (Stanford, Calif.: Stanford University Press, 1991), p. 5.

6 See James Clifford, *The Predicament of Culture: Twentieth-Century Ethnography, Literature, and Art* (Cambridge, Mass.: Harvard University Press, 1988), p. 158.

7 Junichiro Tanizaki, *In Praise of Shadows,* trans. Thomas J. Harper (New Haven, Conn.: Leete's Island Books, 1977), pp. 18–19. I have changed the title in the text to correspond more closely to the Japanese.

8 Roland Barthes, *Empire of Signs,* trans. Richard Howard (New York: Hill and Wang, 1982), p. 4.

9 Simon Leys, *Chinese Shadows* (New York: Penguin Books, 1978), pp. 198–99.

Introduction

1 James Clifford, *The Predicament of Culture: Twentieth-Century Ethnography, Literature, and Art* (Cambridge, Mass.: Harvard University Press, 1988) and Tzvetan Todorov, *On Human Diversity: Nationalism, Racism, and Exoticism in French Thought,* trans. Catherine Porter (Cambridge, Mass.: Harvard University Press, 1993).

2 Edouard Glissant, *Poetics of Relation,* trans. Betsy Wing (Ann Arbor: Uni-

versity of Michigan Press, 1997) and Abdelkebir Khatibi, *Love in Two Languages,* trans. Richard Howard (Minneapolis: University of Minnesota Press, 1990).

3   Jean Bernabé, Patrick Chamoiseau, Raphaël Confiant, *Eloge de la Créolité* (In praise of Creoleness), trans. M. B. Taleb-Khyar (Paris: Gallimard, 1993).

4   *Mercure de France,* 1 March 1955: 385–402, and 1 April 1955: 594–613. This publication did not include the entries for 17 August 1908; 13 January 1909; 28 April 1910; 27 May 1910; Tien-tsin, 2 June 1911; without a date, probably 1912; 8 October 1917; departing from Haïphong; and 2 October 1918, 10 P.M. It also did not include any excerpts from Segalen's correspondence.

5   Victor Segalen, *Essai sur l'exotisme (Notes)* (Paris: Fata Morgana, 1978).

6   Victor Segalen, *Essai sur l'exotisme: Une esthéthique du divers et Textes sur Gauguin et L'Océanie* (Paris: Fata Morgana, 1986). This text contains the same footnotes by Lelong as in the 1978 edition.

7   Victor Segalen, *Essai sur l'exotisme: Une esthétique du divers (Notes)* in *Oeuvres complètes,* 2 vols. (Paris: Laffont, 1995).

Essay on Exoticism

1   Segalen lists here travelers and writers he considers his predecessors. In addition to the medieval traveler, Marco Polo, Segalen refers to three French authors: Jacques-Henri Bernardin de Saint-Pierre (1737–1814), a travel writer and novelist best known for his romance *Paul et Virginie* (1787) set in Mauritius; Vicomte François-René de Chateaubriand (1768–1848) whose travels to America in 1791–92 and to Greece and the Near East in 1806–7 resulted in travel narratives and the novels *Atala, René,* and *Les Natchez;* and Pierre Loti (1850–1923), the pseudonym of Julien Viaud, who was a naval officer and prolific writer of exotic novels. His works are generally comprised of sentimental and erotic interludes set in faraway locales, among them *Aziyadé* (1879), *Rarahu* (1880), and *Madame Chrysenthème* (1888) set in Constantinople, Tahiti, and Japan, respectively.

2   Eugène Fromentin (1820–76), the French novelist, travel writer, artist, and art critic is best known for his novel *Dominique* (1863). Paul Gauguin (1848–1903), painter and grandson of the feminist revolutionary Flora Tristan, lived his later life in Tahiti with the exception of a brief return to France in 1893–95. Segalen arrived in Tahiti in January 1903 and

visited Gauguin's home in Hiva-Oa after the painter's death. In June of the following year Segalen published the article "Gauguin dans son dernier décor" in the *Mercure de France;* his later tribute to the French painter, "Hommage à Gauguin," was published in June 1919, a few weeks after Segalen's death. An additional, unfinished work entitled *Le Maître du Jouir*—so named after Gauguin's cabin which had above the entryway a large carving bearing the words "Maison du Jouir"—was to be a continuation of Segalen's novel *Les Immémoriaux,* with Gauguin serving as the model for the protagonist. See Segalen's reference to this work and to his own celebration of idyllic life in Tahiti in the letter to Henry Manceron, dated 23 September 1911.

3   This is possibly a reference to a book Victor Segalen borrowed from Péan de Pontfilly, a friend and fellow officer aboard *La Durance.* [French edition]

4   Segalen says the symbolist poet Saint-Pol Roux (pseudonym of Paul Roux) *"would* have excelled at this genre," because he was not in fact a traveler. Saint-Pol Roux, born in 1861 in Saint-Henry, near Marseilles, died in Brittany in 1940. It was there that Segalen made his acquaintance through his own childhood friend, Max Prat. Segalen was familiar with Saint-Pol Roux's writings, and Roux was an important link for Segalen to the *Mercure de France* circle, which included writers and critics of the day like Joris-Karl Huysmans and Remy de Gourmont. Segalen participated in a homage to Saint-Pol Roux in February 1909. Their correspondence has been published in France under the title *Saint-Pol Roux—Victor Segalen. Correspondance* (Limonges: Rougerie, 1975).

5   Segalen may be thinking here of Paul Claudel's *Connaissance de l'Est,* a collection of prose poems which he greatly admired. Claudel (1868–1955) was a diplomat, poet, and dramatist who spent some sixteen years in the Far East, mostly in China. Segalen met him only in 1914. Segalen's prose poem collection, *Stèles,* is dedicated to Paul Claudel.

6   Segalen's ethnographic novel, *Les Immémoriaux,* was published in 1907. In it he narrates the interactions between the Maoris and the missionaries through the eyes of a Maori protagonist, Térii, who is the repository of the Maoris' oral tradition.

7   These are examples of texts which subvert the usual relation between subject and object, providing the reader with an unusual (nonhuman) perspective. Kipling's *Jungle Books* opens with the animals' discovery of Mowgli, the "man cub." The stories "The Ship that Found Herself" and

".007"—both in the collection *The Day's Work*—narrate adventures on sea and on land as told by a ship and a locomotive, respectively.

8   The term "Bovarysm" refers to Gustave Flaubert's novel *Madame Bovary* (1856), whose central character, Emma Bovary, a romantic dreamer, continually conjures up visions of exotic lands and material objects to satisfy her longings. Segalen does not use the term in a pejorative sense, however. Instead, he takes it from Jules de Gaultier's work *Le Bovarysme* where it is used to articulate the subject's essential alterity. Segalen uses this concept to argue that diversity lies at the very core of the individual, who imagines himself/herself as an other. This, for him, constitutes an "essential exoticism," and serves to reassure him (as expressed in the later entries) that difference and diversity will not become extinct despite the decline of exoticism.

9   Maurice Maeterlink (1862–1949) was a Belgian symbolist poet, dramatist, and essayist. Born in Ghent, he lived mostly in France after 1890. Apart from his poetic output, he is remembered particularly for his play *Pelléas et Mélisande* (1892) which was set to music by Claude Debussy and performed in 1902.

10 Herbert George Wells (1866–1946) is known for his scientific romances. Many of these—including *The Time Machine, The Wonderful Visit, The Island of Doctor Moreau,* and *The War of the Worlds*—had already been translated (along with his nonfictional writings such as *Discovery of the Future*) into French at the time of this entry.

11 The sheet upon which this entry was written was attached to the first entry of *Essay on Exoticism,* dated 9 June 1908. [French Edition]

12 The word *exot* is invented by Segalen to refer to those persons possessing a great capacity for experiencing diversity and hence exoticism. Others, like Loti, are referred to as "pseudo-Exots."

13 Use of the French subject pronoun "*tu*" suggests here an informality or intimacy between the Exot and the Exotic.

14 Max Prat was a friend of Segalen's since childhood.

15 Segalen was working on a drama titled *Orphée-roi* that Debussy was considering setting to music. The project seems to have been suggested by Debussy, who had rejected Segalen's earlier drama *Siddhartâ* but liked what Segalen had done with the character of Orpheus in a short story titled "Voix mortes: Musiques Maori" (which Segalen had sent to him unsolicited). From Claude Debussy's letters to Segalen and from an account of their collaboration by Debussy's close friend, Louis Laloy, it

seems that enthusiasm for the project lay primarily on Segalen's side, and the drama was never set to music by Debussy. In his memoir *La Musique retrouvée, 1902–1927* (Paris: Plon, 1928), Laloy writes: "We made the acquaintance of Victor Segalen, whose intellectual research was interesting but as far as could possibly be from any kind of music, and especially Debussy's. Since he seemed very nice, however, my friend did not dare thwart him and lost much time discussing the text of *Orphée-roi* with him, continually correcting and revising it. . . . Without diminishing the merit of the author, one must acknowledge that he was for Debussy a problem, or, rather, an unsolvable enigma" (175).

16 Segalen completed this short story, whose protagonist is an old Maori man, in 1908. It is included, together with two articles on Gauguin, in the most recent French edition of *Essai sur l'exotisme* (Paris: Fata Morgana, 1986).

17 This list includes the names of the other contributors to this projected volume, all writers of colonial literature: Marius-Ary Leblond—the pseudonym used by Georges Athenas and Aimé Merlo, who were born in Reunion Island—wrote many colonial novels and short stories as well as works of literary criticism on colonial literature; Pierre Mille (1864–1941) is best known for his stories about the adventures and misadventures of a simple colonial soldier named Barnavaux; Robert Randau, pseudonym of Robert Arnaud (1873–1950), a writer born in Algeria, is the author of several novels set in Algeria and French West Africa, among which *Les Colons* is most often noted by critics of the period; John-Antoine Nau (1860–1918) is the author of *Cristobal le poète* (1906); and Louis Bertrand (1866–1941) is the author of literary and historical studies, travel accounts, and novels such as *Le Sang des races* (1899) and *La Cina* (1901). He taught in a high school in Algeria from 1891 to 1900. The publishing house Calmann-Lévy proposed a collection of colonial tales to be grouped under the title *Les Exotiques.* Colonial literature was emerging as an important genre in the early decades of the twentieth century and becoming a subject of interest for literary critics of the time. This project, however, was never completed. In its title, the would-be collection reveals precisely the confusion between the colonial and the exotic that Segalen saw as detrimental to the survival of the exotic, since the collection was to include works by colonial writers. See his view on the subject in the entry dated 8 October 1917.

18 *Les Soirées de Médan* is the title of a volume of naturalist short stories

by Emile Zola, Paul Alexis, Henry Céard, Léon Hennique, Joris-Karl Huysmans, and Guy de Maupassant, published in France in 1880. It was named after Zola's country home near Paris and gained prominence as a showcase of naturalist writing.

19   Paul Bonnetain (1858–99) was a travel writer and novelist who published various works based on his travels to the Far East. These include *Au Tonkin* (1885), *L'Extrême Orient* (1887), and *Amours nomades* (1888). Jean Ajalbert (1863–1947) wrote similar travel sketches, among them *Sous le sabre* (1898), *Paysages de femmes* (1887), *Sur le vif* (1886), and *L'Auvergne* (1897). Their writings are likely the kind of impressionistic works Segalen is frequently critical of in *Essay on Exoticism*.

20   H. Oldenberg was a professor at the University of Kiel, Germany. The second edition of his work, *Le Bouddha,* was translated from the German and published in France in 1894. It is a general overview of the Buddha's life, doctrine, and disciples. Segalen was probably also familiar with Oldenberg's *La Religion du Véda,* which was published in a French translation in 1903.

21   Charles de Secondat, Baron de Montesquieu (1689–1755) was a political philosopher and novelist best known for his epistolary novel *Les lettres Persanes* (1721) and for *L'Esprit des lois* (1748), a lengthy treatise on the general principles and historical origins of laws.

22   Jules de Gaultier (1858–1942) is the author of *Le Bovarysme.* He was an important popularizer of German thought (especially of Nietzsche's) in France in the late nineteenth and early twentieth century.

23   René Quinton (1867–1925) was a French physiologist. He is best known for his work *L'Eau de mer, milieu organique,* where he reveals a similarity between plasma and sea water, and draws some therapeutic applications from this discovery. Quinton plasma — sea water that is sterilized and diluted with distilled water in such a way as to approximate human plasma — bears his name. Segalen, who was trained as a doctor, was interested in both the medical and philosophical aspects of Quinton's work. [French Edition]

24   This passage from Clouard is added in the margins of the text, no doubt after he read Henri Clouard's article, "Maurice de Guérin et le sentiment de la nature," which was published in the *Mercure de France* on 1 January 1909. [French Edition] It is discussed further in the letter to Jeanne Perdriel-Vaissière, dated 7 January 1909 and in the entry dated January or February 1909.

25　"Veda," the Sanskrit word for knowledge, is the name given to the four
　　sacred texts of the Hindus: the Rigveda, the Samaveda, the Yajurveda,
　　and the Atharvaveda. They are understood to have been revealed to
　　humans by the divinities and to contain all divine knowledge.

26　Louis Bertrand published several articles in the *Revue des Deux Mondes* at
　　about the time of this entry, but Victor Segalen is surely referring to the
　　one titled "Le Mirage Oriental" in the 15 September 1908 issue: 353–75. In
　　this article, Bertrand expresses sentiments similar to those of Segalen: he
　　criticizes skewed and superficial visions of the Orient, especially the use
　　of the Orient (by Westerners) as no more than "local color" or "scenic
　　backdrop." For these tendencies, he blames both past literary accounts
　　of the Orient (specifically Victor Hugo's *Les Orientales)* and contempo-
　　rary modes of travel. The latter, by providing comfort and displacement
　　with ease and rapidity, prevents travelers from coming into contact with
　　the realities of their destinations. They become passive viewers who sat-
　　isfy themselves with picturesque scenes. He ends the article by recom-
　　mending a way of traveling capable of correcting this stunted vision of
　　the Western traveler. A sequel article by Bertrand, published in the same
　　journal on 1 November 1908: 139–72, continues and somewhat extends
　　the argument of the first installment.

27　Segalen's short story, "Dans un monde sonor," explores just such an idea:
　　it tells the story of a man who lives solely in a world of sound. The story
　　was first published in the *Mercure de France* on 16 August 1907.

28　The phrase "[a]nd he rejoices in his Diversity" comes from Jules de
　　Gaultier's *Le Bovarysme.* It is quoted twice more in this work, notably at
　　the very end of *Essay on Exoticism.*

29　Louis Laloy (1874–1944) was a French musicologist and critic. His inter-
　　ests included the music of the Far East and of Ancient Greece. He was
　　also a defender of contemporary French music, a close friend of both
　　Ravel and Debussy, and the author of the first major work on Debussy.
　　Segalen saw himself as sharing, no doubt, an interest in the Far East
　　and in China in particular, as Laloy both lectured on and wrote about
　　Chinese music.

30　This is Segalen's imagined catalog entry of the essay he is writing, and
　　it projects that the essay will be published in ten years. Max Anély is the
　　pseudonym under which Segalen published some of his earlier writings.

31　This is a quotation from Jules de Gaultier's "Introduction à la vie intel-
　　lectuelle" which appeared in the *Revue Blanche,* 1 Dec. 1895: 508–14. The

emphasis is Segalen's. [French Edition] The full paragraph reads as follows:

> Nonetheless, the wise man resists this propensity for turning his
> enthusiasms into beliefs. Knowing that it is never legitimate to sup-
> port these, he recommences, with his foot in intellectual soil this
> time; he recognizes the necessity of taking a particular liking for
> something as a principle of certainty. And, in the space of an in-
> stant, he conceives of his desire as the center of the universe; he
> is all too aware of the passionate origin of the theory which has
> overwhelmed him. This is how he recognizes its relativity, its ties,
> its limits; he knows the precise place where this theory has broken
> the chain of causality to attain his support by leaning on his will;
> having thus isolated it, he can survey the terrain, and, freed from
> the desire to reside in that coveted palace, he nonetheless sees its
> order and its organization with a disinterested joy. Thus the normal
> relation between an intellect and whatever work of the will—that
> of the spectator to the representation—is reestablished (512–13).

32   Segalen's initial sense of his own vision as one among many, as no more
and no less valid than any other vision, undergoes a change in the course
of the dated entries which compose this essay. His entry for 21 April 1917
states that, while he initially thought his essay represented simply his
own way of thinking, he now believes that his theory of exoticism has
general validity. He then goes on to discuss the ironic situation whereby
his realization of his theory's validity coincides with the decline of exoticism in the world.

33   This phrase is repeated at the end of the entry dated 2 October 1918,
10 P.M., where it is no longer in quotation marks.

34   This is a quote from Jules de Gaultier's "Des fondements de l'incertitude
en matière d'opinion," which appeared in the *Revue Blanche* on 15 January
1896. [French Edition] The article is based on Kant's *Critique of Pure Reason,* and the quotation Segalen selects comes under the heading "Physiological Aspects" in de Gaultier's article. De Gaultier is discussing the
internal division of the subject here, arguing that unity can only represent itself to itself through diversity. This notion repeats and slightly
reformulates his concept of Bovarysm.

35   These are quotations from de Gaultier's "Des fondements de l'incertitude en matière d'opinion" discussed in the preceding note.

36   Edouard Schuré (1841–1929) is the author of *La Vie mystique* (1894) and

Les Grands initiés (1889). The latter work is a study of the occult which attempts to reconcile science and religion, a dualism Schuré deemed destructive for civilization. This is one kind of synthesis in Schuré's writing; another can be seen in his fusion of all ages and cultures in *Les Grands initiés,* which is organized around the figures of Rama, Krishna, Hermes, Moses, Orpheus, Pythagoras, Plato, and Jesus. Joséphin Péladan (1859–1918), also known as "Sâr Péladan," was a playwright and author of mystical dramas. He participated in a revival of Rosicrucianism in the late nineteenth century, and his salons were the center of Rosicrucianism for a time. In 1890 he founded the Théâtre de la Rose-Croix.

37 Segalen is referring to a theory put forth by René Quinton, who asserted the Law of Constancy in biological studies as against Darwin's theory of evolution. Quinton concluded that a law of intellectual constancy also existed.

38 A friend of the Segalen family. [French Edition]

39 Henri Clouard, "Maurice de Guérin et le sentiment de la nature," *Le Mercure de France,* 1 January 1909: 34–45. Maurice de Guérin (1810–39) was a disciple of the Christian democrat and writer Lamennais. De Guérin formed part of a community at La Chesnaie, where he developed a strong affinity for nature. He is chiefly known for his prose poem *Le Centaure,* first published posthumously in 1840 and for his *Journal intime* (also called *Le Cahier vert*) which is full of romantic and religious evocations of the natural world. Segalen refers to these two works in his discussion of Clouard's work on Maurice de Guérin.

40 These pages were not dated by Segalen but were probably written shortly after he read Clouard's article on Maurice de Guérin. [French Edition]

41 Segalen is quoting his own words from the section entitled "The Exoticism of Nature" in the entry dated 11 December 1908.

42 Segalen refers to Jean-Jacques Rousseau (1712–78) and George Sand (1804–76) with reference, most probably, to their descriptions of idyllic nature.

43 The structural similarity Segalen refers to in the phrases *"sentiment de la nature"* and *"Exotisme de la nature"* is lost in translation.

44 Here and elsewhere, the italicized words are Segalen's emphases. Segalen sometimes quotes imprecisely from Clouard's article, although without distorting Clouard's meaning.

45 This is probably a reference to Maurice de Guérin's return to secular life after the community at La Chesnaie was dissolved in 1833. It was there

that he had become aware of nature and filled with a deep affection for it. In Paris he struggled to survive by the pen, then fell ill with tuberculosis and died.

46   Victor Hugo (1802–85), a poet, dramatist, and novelist, was a central figure in the Romantic movement in France. Segalen is likely referring to Hugo's poetry, as in the volumes *Feuilles d'automne* (1831), *Les Chants du crépuscule* (1835), and *Les Rayons et les ombres* (1840). George Sand (1804–76) was the author of romantic and idyllic novels often dealing with social concerns, and frequently set in the countryside. Some of these, such as *La Mare au diable* (1846), *La Petite Fadette* (1848), and *François le champi* (1850), celebrate rustic life.

47   De Guérin's prose poem "Le Centaure" has Mélampe, a young centaur, as its narrator. He tells of his encounter with the aged centaur Chiron, who in turn recounts his early days and lonely later years. Segalen is comparing Mélampe's narration—which provides us with the perspective of a centaur—to that of Térii, the young Maori man in *Les Immémoriaux* through whose eyes we view the changes taking place in the Maori community as a result of the arrival of European missionaries.

48   Alphonse de Lamartine (1790–1869) is a romantic poet and author of *Méditations poétiques* (1820), a collection of twenty-four odes and elegies (the well-known "Le Lac" and "L'Isolement" among them). These poems express an appreciation for nature as an expression of the poet's own mournful mood. Clouard is likely referring to such poems when he speaks of Lamartine's use of nature as "a pretext."

49   The words in parentheses are Segalen's gloss of Clouard's discussion.

50   André Chénier (1762–94) is a pre-romantic poet of the eighteenth century who was executed during the Terror.

51   Clouard may be thinking of Goethe's *Sorrows of Young Werther,* where the protagonist continually expresses his love of nature in lengthy romantic passages. Here too, nature is, by and large, a reflection of the subjective moods of a melancholy narrator.

52   Nature is a feminine noun in French, a fact Clouard uses to play up the motif of union, passion, or love between it and Maurice de Guérin.

53   Segalen's article, "Le Double Rimbaud," was published in the *Mercure de France* on 15 April 1906. In it he writes: "Lovers would be horrified if—at the height of their shared pleasure, when a joy spreads over them that is so common to both that the two proclaim their union—they could grasp the unbridgeable barrier which separates two sentient beings, and which

will always separate them despite the seeming harmony of their unique joy." [French Edition] Here and elsewhere, Segalen is fascinated by the notion of an intimate knowledge of a single entity which nonetheless contains essential difference. This concept is central to his conception of exoticism, which involves moments of immersion and understanding, followed by distance and objectivity. As such, the (exotic) object always remains exotic, never merges with the subject, a subject who, at any rate, is also different from itself. Segalen refers to his study of the French poet Arthur Rimbaud (1854–91) precisely because he, Segalen, is captivated by the existence of two seemingly very different people in one being: on the one hand, the poet, author of *Le Bateau ivre* (1871) and *Les Illuminations* (1886), and, on the other hand, after abandoning literature, an explorer and trader. During his travels Segalen had interviewed various people who knew the poet in his later phase, after he had arrived in Djibouti, in French Somaliland.

54 Etienne Pivert de Senancour (1770–1846) is best known for his novel *Obermann* (1804), a novel of romantic introspection filled with descriptions of nature. Much like *The Sorrows of Young Werther*, it is epistolary, comprised of letters written by the unhappy hero who can experience no joy in the world, but who finds some comfort in the beauty of nature. Henri Frédéric Amiel (1821–81) is best known for his diary, published posthumously under the title *Fragments d'un journal intime*.

55 Segalen is likely summarizing a passage from de Guérin's *Journal* rather than quoting exactly. The passage closest to the one quoted here reads: "An infinite number of details have escaped me, but their impression remains precious to me. This impression has redoubled my attraction for observing nature and has made me lean toward its inexhaustible well of consolations and poetry" (Paris: Gallimard 1984), p. 100.

56 The exclamation mark is added by Segalen.

57 Marius-Ary Leblond's novel, *L'Oued*—so called after the name of a river in North Africa—was published in 1907. It tells the story of Ambroise, a young French woman who has left the convent to join her father, a colonial administrator in Algeria. There she experiences various epiphanies prompted largely by the landscape's beauty and is pursued by three suitors: an Algerian nationalist, her father's assistant colonial administrator, and the indigenous Belkassem. The novel focuses on the French girl's perspective, hence that of the French colonial.

58 The policy of associationism emerged in the early twentieth century as

a successor to assimilationist policies. Associationism, while still hier-
archical in nature, promoted some flexibility in colonial administration
by paying particular attention to the cultural and ethnic differences of
each colony as they related to its governance and by encouraging greater
cooperation with native inhabitants. Assimilationist policies were more
centralized across France's diverse colonial possessions and gave less
power to local colonial administrators. See Raymond F. Betts's work
on French colonial policies, *Assimilation and Association in French Colonial
Theory 1890–1914* (New York: Columbia University Press, 1961).

59   Segalen's article "Les Synesthésies et l'Ecole symboliste" was published
in the *Mercure de France* in April 1902. [French Edition]

60   Joris-Karl Huysmans (1848–1907) is a French novelist often associated
with decadent literature of the fin de siècle.

61   Marc Logé gives a biography of Hearn (b. Greece 1850–d. Japan 1904)
in this article and discusses Hearn's work. He mentions a work titled
Kwaidan, ou histoires et études de choses étranges, a book of Japanese legends
which ends with three studies of insects, of which two (studies of Japan's
butterflies and of ants) had already appeared in the *Mercure de France.* The
third study was on mosquitoes. It is probably in this journal that Segalen
read of Hearn's discussion of ants, as Marc Logé's translation of *Kwaidan*
appeared only in 1910.

62   This note is written on the back of the note dated 24 December 1908.
[French Edition]

63   Pierre Corneille's play, *Le Cid,* was first produced in 1637. It is a tragedy
set in Seville, Spain. The fables of Jean de La Fontaine (1621–95) set the
fables of Aesop, Phaedrus, Horace, and other ancient sources to French
verse.

64   Segalen undertook two archaeological expeditions with Auguste Gilbert
de Voisins in China: the first in 1909, and the second, with Jean Lartigue
as well, in 1914.

65   Robert Louis Stevenson's *Kidnapped* was translated into French by Albert
Savine in 1905.

66   Augusto is a nickname for Auguste Gilbert de Voisins. [French Edition]

67   Segalen's published manuscript, *Feuilles de route,* contains the following
description of the "defensive measures" taken at the Tomb of Hongwu in
Nanking. The description is dated 16 March 1917, approximately seven
years after this entry was written.

[This is] my third voyage to the tomb, whose portico pavilion, with its stele-doorway adorned with turtles, and its red mausoleum, is visible from Pei-Ki Ko and from anywhere in the Chinese village.

My three visits witnessed successive stages of disgrace. On the first visit, in 1909 (May), the Beasts and the monuments were abandoned, in ruins, in a removed site, which was wild despite springtime. In the second visit (1910), the viceroy and protector Toan-fang . . . had a six-line stele constructed on which he had requested that visitors refrain from damaging the pitiful, wood balustrades painted red, which were there to 'fend off' and to protect the Beasts—like the butcher's grille protects his meats... (but, very quickly, this balustrade had only three sides, then two sides...).

Today the red railings are gone. The six-line stele remains. In a yet more unfortunate state, the Beasts have also remained there!

These now comprise the most pitiful testimony to Ming Statuary. (See *Oeuvres complètes,* vol.1 [Paris: Laffont, 1995], p. 1205.)

68 The Ming dynasty is the penultimate Imperial dynasty and lasted from 1368–1644. Its capital was first Nanking, then, after 1421, Peking. The Ching Dynasty (1644–1911) is the last Imperial dynasty and is of a Manchurian origin.

69 K'ang-hi art was produced during the reign of the Ching emperor K'ang-hi, that is, between 1662–1723.

70 Henri Bouvelet's work was published in May 1910, just months before Segalen's entry. In his preface, Bouvelet speaks of the uniqueness of each individuality and opposes positivist science "which tends more and more to prove to us that what we call a difference in quality is never anything but the result of a dissimilarity in quantity." *Le Royaume de la Terre* (Paris: La Belle Edition, 1910), p. viii.

71 This note was not dated by Segalen. The reference to the stele poem "Conseil au bon voyageur" allows us to situate its composition around 1911. [French Edition]

72 "Advice to the Discerning Traveler" is the title of a poem in Segalen's *Stèles.*

73 Jules Boissière (1863–97) died in Hanoi. He published three works during his lifetime: *Devant l'Enigme* (1883), *Provensa* (1885), and his traveler's impressions of the Far East, *Fumeurs d'Opium* (1896). His poetry collection *Les Goélands—Li Gabian* in Provençal (the text is a bilingual edition with the French facing the Provençal text)—was published posthumously. Segalen refers to Boissière as a "*félibre*" and to his beautiful

poetry as written in *"vers félibriens."* *Félibre* was a movement for the resto-
ration of Provençal as a living language in the mid-nineteenth century.
The movement was created by seven Provençal poets — the best-known
among them is Frédéric Mistral (1830–1914) — who called themselves *Félibres*. While Jules Boissière was not among them, he was influenced by
this movement to revive the use of the Provençal tongue.

74   I have restored here the correct version of this line from the poem "Lou
Serventés" in *Li Gabian* (Avignoun: J. Roumanille, 1899), p. 58–59.

75   "Lou Bouddha" ("Le Bouddha") and "Cementèri d'Annam" ("Cimetière
d'Annam") are both poems from Boissière's collection *Li Gabian*. (See
preceding note.) The former describes a battle scene and the Buddha's
serene, indifferent face (114–15); the latter narrates a vision of the waking
dead in the cemetery as well as the narrator's realization of his isolation
from both the dead the and living (130–31).

76   These are verses from the poem "Lou Felibre raconto" ("Le Félibre ran-
conte"), pp. 170–71.

77   These verse lines appear in a later poem also titled "Lou Felibre raconto,"
pp. 178–79.

78   Emile Nolly (b. 1880) was a writer of colonial fiction.

79   Anatole France is the pseudonym of Jacques-Anatole-François Thibault
(1844–1924), a novelist and critic. Segalen may be thinking of France's
novel *Thaïs* (1890) which is set in Egypt in the fourth century A.D.

80   Claude Farrère is the pseudonym of Frédéric Bargone (1876–1957). He
was a naval officer who, following Loti, wrote many novels set in exotic
locales: *Les Civilisés* (1905) was set in Saigon, *L'Homme qui assassine* (1907) in
Constantinople, and *La Bataille* (1911) in Japan. Through Farrère, Segalen
met Auguste Gilbert de Voisins.

81   Edmond (1822–96) and Jules (1830–70) Goncourt are naturalist writers
best known for their novel *Germinie Lacerteux* (1864) and for their *Journal,*
begun in 1851.

82   *Les Xipéhuz* is a novella written by Joseph-Henry Rosny (1856–1940) and
Séraphin-Justin Rosny (1859–1948) and published in 1910. The tale is a
curious one, telling of the invasion of strange 'forms' (cylinders, cones,
etc.) called the Xipéhuz, who threaten the existence of humans. One
individual named Bakhoun is finally able to devise a plan to annihi-
late the Xipéhuz after studying their civilization at length. He is successful, but after the last Xipéhuz is killed, Bakhoun laments their disappearance: "And I buried my head in my hands, and a cry surged up

from my heart. For now that the *xipéhuz* have succumbed, my heart missed them, and I asked the Unique One what Fatality wished for all the splendor of Life to be sullied by Murder's Shadows!" (Paris: Mercure de France, 1910), p. 142. The work reads as an allegory of colonialism, and its frequent use of neologisms—of which Segalen is highly critical—is partly due to the imagined and fantastic nature of the text's subject. Segalen's quotations from this text are from pages 38, 46, and 48, respectively.

83 The neologism Segalen complains of is the word *"massement"* in French (*Les Xipéhuz,* 9). It is translated here into "massing."

84 *Les Xipéhuz,* pp. 13–14. The emphasis is Segalen's.

85 Henry Manceron is a childhood friend of Segalen's.

86 La Manche is a region in northwest France.

87 Segalen left France for Tahiti in October 1902, arrived in Tahiti in January 1903, and left Tahiti for France in September 1904.

88 Segalen idealizes the attributes of the young girl or young virgin elsewhere as well. See his poem "Eloge de la jeune fille" (In praise of the young girl) in *Stèles.*

89 This historical novel about the Son of Heaven was published posthumously in 1975. The novel is both about the last adult emperor and the mythical dimension of this personage. The Son of Heaven is the designation given to the Chinese emperor.

90 The first edition of *Stèles* was published in August 1912. Sixteen new "steles" were published a year later in the *Mercure de France* and were included in the second, 1914 edition of the text. A stele is an upright slab or pillar of stone bearing an inscription. These traditional Chinese monuments were used to honor notable individuals or mark an event, and could be found in such places as temple courtyards, in front of tombs, and by the roadside. See Michael Taylor's discussion of the publication of this work in his "Translator's Note" to *Steles.* While the work makes use of Segalen's knowledge and study of many Chinese steles, it is by no means a simple translation of them. Segalen was inspired by these historical monuments and their inscriptions to create his own poetic voices and narratives. Manceron's suggestion that he might look to the work of Louÿs or Mérimée (see the note immediately below) suggests that Segalen was at some point searching for the best way to present and to position himself vis-à-vis his steles, opting finally for ambiguity.

91 Pierre Louÿs (1870–1925) is the pseudonym of Pierre Louis. He was a

novelist and poet. Manceron may be suggesting Segalen seek out the example of Louÿs' *Chansons de Bilitis* (1894), a collection of prose love poems that Louÿs claimed were translations from a Greek poetess and contemporary of Sappho, when in fact they were not. He deceived many readers and scholars. Prosper Mérimée (1803–70) was a novelist, archaeologist, and historian. He served as Inspector General of Historical Monuments from 1834, a fact which may have linked his endeavors to Segalen's archaeological interest in China in Manceron's mind.

92   The reference is to Segalen's poem "Perdre le midi quotidien," which he was revising that September.

93   Reference is to the poem "Sans marque de règne," the first poem in the section of *Stèles* entitled "Stèles face au midi."

94   This is the second law of thermodynamics. My thanks to Salomeia Schlick for her scientific explanation of this law.

95   See note 1 for information regarding Bernardin de Saint-Pierre.

96   Maurice Barrès (1862–1923), a novelist, essayist, and politician, was born in La Lorraine and then moved to Paris.

97   André Gide (1869–1951) writes this in his article "Chronique de l'Ermitage. Seconde visite de l'interviewer," which first appeared in early 1905 in the symbolist review *L'Ermitage* and was later reprinted in the volume *Nouveaux prétextes* (1911). The very first ellipsis is Gide's, but the remaining ones are Segalen's, as he condenses four paragraphs of Gide's article into the short passage cited here. (*Nouveaux prétextes* [Paris: Mercure de France, 1911]), pp. 59–60.

98   Pierre Richard was a friend Segalen met in Bordeaux at the Ecole de Santé Navale. They met again in China in 1911. [French Edition]

99   "Le Génie de Flaubert" by Jules de Gaultier was published in two parts in the *Mercure de France:* the first appeared on 16 November 1912: 225–60; the second on 1 December 1912: 490–526. The passage Segalen uses here appears on page 255 of the first installment. He replaces the word "error" with the word "diversity." The emphasis is his.

100   *The Princesse de Clèves* by Madame de Lafayette—considered by some to be the first novel ever written—was published in 1678. *Salammbô* by Gustave Flaubert was published in 1862. It is set in ancient Carthage after the first Punic war.

101   Segalen's *Peintures* is a collection of prose pieces written as a narrator's commentary on imaginary paintings to an audience. It was published in 1916.

102 The poems in *Stèles* were each contained within a rectangular, outlined space, mimicking the concrete and timeless quality which Segalen attributed to the steles he saw in China.

103 These are critics and literary historians. Best known among them are Désiré Nisard (1806–88), author of *L'Histoire de la littérature française* (1855–61), and Gustave Lanson (1857–1934), whose influential *Histoire de la littérature française* was first published in 1894 and then appeared in many successive editions.

104 "Patters" captures the conversational tone of *Peintures,* whereas "Parade of Easels" conveys the exhibition of paintings and the narrative progression from one painting to the next which structures the prose poem collection *Peintures.* The text was composed between 1911 and 1916. The word "parade" is highlighted at the very opening of the text, where the narrator addresses his audience: "You are there: you wait, decided perhaps to listen to me right until the end; but destined or not to see clearly, without modesty, to see it all right up until the end?—I do not in any way exact promises: I do not wish for any reply or help but only for your silence and your eyes. First, have you any idea of what is shown here and why this PARADE takes place?" See *Paintings,* trans. Andrew Harvey and Iain Watson (London: Quartet Books, 1991), p. 1. I have slightly modified this translation.

105 Riquette is the nickname for Henry Manceron's wife, Marie. [French Edition]

106 Jean Lartigue (b. 1886) participated in this expedition to China that began in February 1914. Segalen had first met him in China in 1909.

107 See Friedrich Nietzsche's *Thus Spoke Zarathustra.*

108 This latter quote is from the section in *Peintures* entitled "Trône chancelant de la maison de Hsia." See "Quaking Throne of the House of Hsia" in *Paintings,* 102–5.

109 The poet and essayist Charles Péguy (1873–1914) died leading his company at the battle of the Marne in World War I. He was, by then, an ardent patriot and nationalist.

110 This entry was written during the time of the Russian Revolution. Segalen, while admiring the revolutionaries' courage, was sorry that the tsar had not exerted greater force to suppress them. Segalen's regret at the passing away of Imperial China is expressed strongly in his novel *René Leys,* set during the time of the Chinese revolution in 1911.

111 It would have seemed unpatriotic to minimize the importance of break-

ing through the Hindenburg line in 1917. The Allied forces succeeded in this endeavor only in September 1918.

112   The editors of the 1978 edition of *Essai sur l'exotisme* note that these seven groupings represent different files into which Segalen apparently planned to classify his various entries on exoticism, remarking that they may represent chapter headings he planned for the final version of this work.

113   Joseph-Arthur, Comte de Gobineau (1816–62) wrote his *Essai sur l'inégalité des races humaines* from 1853 to 1855. Segalen was no doubt drawn to Gobineau's notion that degeneration results from the intermixing of races, whereby, according to Gobineau, each race loses those qualities and values intrinsic to it. This notion echoes Segalen's concept of exoticism and of diversity, both of which value the preservation and maintenance of difference, be it cultural, sexual, economic, or political. See Tzvetan Todorov's discussion of Gobineau's conception of race in *On Human Diversity: Nationalism, Racism, and Exoticism in French Thought,* trans. Catherine Porter (Cambridge, Mass.: Harvard University Press, 1993), pp. 129–40.

*Other Works by Victor Segalen
Available in English*

The Great Statuary of China. Chicago: University of Chicago Press, 1978. A translation by Eleanor Levieux of *Chine: La Grande Statuaire*.

A Lapse of Memory. Brisbane: Boombana Publications, 1995. A translation by Rosemary Arnoux of *Les Immémoriaux*.

René Leys. Woodstock, NY: Overlook Press, 1988. A translation by J. A. Underwood of *René Leys*.

Paintings. London: Quartet Books, 1991. A translation by Andrew Harvey and Iain Watson of *Peintures*.

Steles. London: Jonathan Cape, 1990. A translation by Andrew Harvey and Iain Watson of *Stèles*.

Steles. Santa Monica, Calif.: Lapis Press, 1987. A translation by Michael Taylor of *Stèles*.

Stelae. Santa Barbara, Calif.: Unicorn Press, 1969. A translation by Nathaniel Tarn of twenty-six of the sixty-four poems in *Stèles*.

Selected Critical Works
on Victor Segalen in English

Arnoux, Rosemary. "Victor Segalen: Ethnography and '*Exotisme*' in *Les Im-mémoriaux*." *AUMLA* 82 (1994): 49–65.

Bartkowski, Frances. "Time and the Traveler: Victor Segalen's *Exoticism*." In *Travelers, Immigrants, Inmates: Essays in Estrangement*. Minneapolis: University of Minnesota Press, 1995.

Bongie, Chris. *Exotic Memories: Literature, Colonialism, and the Fin de Siècle*. Stanford, Calif.: Stanford University Press, 1991.

Clifford, James. "A Poetics of Displacement: Victor Segalen." In *The Predicament of Culture: Twentieth-Century Ethnography, Literature, and Art*. Cambridge, Mass.: Harvard University Press, 1988.

Forsdick, Charles. "*Fin-d-siècle* Exoticism: Reading Victor Segalen in the 1990s." *French Studies Bulletin* 60 (1996): 13–16.

———. "*Honorons le temps dans sa voracité:* Weathering the Exotic in the Work of Victor Segalen." *Romance Studies,* no. 17 (1999): 1–13.

Hsieh, Yvonne Y. *From Occupation to Revolution: China through the Eyes of Loti, Claudel, Segalen, and Malraux (1895–1933)*. Birmingham, Ala.: Summa, 1996.

——— *Victor Segalen's Literary Encounter with China: Chinese Moulds, Western Thoughts*. Toronto: University of Toronto Press, 1988.

Michel, Andreas. "En Route to the Other: Victor Segalen's *Essai sur l'exotisme* and *Equipée*." *Romance Studies,* no. 16 (1990): 21–30.

———. "The Subject of Exoticism: Victor Segalen's *Equipée*." *Surfaces* 61 (1996): 1–32.

Quach, Gianna. "Shadow Plays: *René Leys* and the Exotic Quest." *L'Esprit Créateur* 34 (1994): 92–101.

Schlick, Yaël. "On the Persistence of a Concept: Victor Segalen's *René Leys* and the Death(s) of Exoticism." *Australian Journal of French Studies* 35 (1998): 199–214.

———. "Re-Writing the Exotic: Mille, Segalen, and the Emergence of *littérature coloniale." Dalhousie French Studies* 35 (1996): 123–34.

Todorov, Tzvetan. "Segalen." In *On Human Diversity: Nationalism, Racism, and Exoticism in French Thought.* Trans. Catherine Porter. Cambridge, Mass.: Harvard University Press, 1993.

Index

Victor Segalen (1878–1919) was an innovative poet,
novelist, and essayist whose works include *A Lapse of
Memory*, *Steles*, *Paintings*, and *The Great Statuary of China*.
A naval doctor, he traveled widely through Polynesia
and China, where he undertook two archaeological
expeditions. He died in 1919 in his native Brittany. The
majority of his works have been published posthumously.

Yaël Rachel Schlick is an Assistant Adjunct Professor
at Queen's University in Canada. She has written on
nineteenth- and twentieth-century fiction, colonial
literature, and travel writing.

Library of Congress Cataloging-in-Publication Data
Segalen, Victor, 1878–1919.
[Essai sur l'exotisme. English]
Essay on exoticism : an aesthetics of diversity / Victor
Segalen ; translated and edited by Yaël Rachel Schlick ;
foreword by Harry Harootunian.
p. cm. — (Post-contemporary interventions)
Includes index.
ISBN 0-8223-2810-0 (cloth : alk. paper)
ISBN 0-8223-2822-4 (pbk. : alk. paper)
1. Aesthetics. 2. Difference (Philosophy) I. Schlick,
Yaël Rachel II. Title. III. Series.
BH39 .S4413 2002   111'.85—dc21   2001042537